THE ART OF UTOPIA

THE ART OF UTOPIA

A New Direction in Contemporary Aboriginal Art

Michael Boulter

CRAFTSMAN HOUSE

First published in 1991 by Craftsman House BVI Ltd, Tortola, BVI
Distributed in Australia by Craftsman House,
20 Barcoo Street,
Roseville East, NSW 2069, Australia

Distributed internationally through the following offices:

USA	**UK**	**ASIA**
STBS Ltd.	STBS Ltd.	STBS (Singapore) Pte Ltd
PO Box 786	5th Floor, Reading Bridge House	Kent Ridge PO Box 1180
Cooper Station	Reading Bridge Approach	PO Box 1180
New York	Reading RG1 8PP	Singapore 9111
NY 10276	England	Republic of Singapore

ISBN 976 8097 15 9

Design   *Sue Edmonds*
Typesetter   *Netan Pty Limited, Sydney*
Printer   *Kyodo, Singapore*

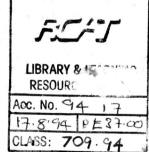

THIS BOOK
IS DEDICATED TO
THE ARTISTS OF UTOPIA
AND THEIR FAMILIES

TABLE OF CONTENTS

ACKNOWLEDGEMENTS

This book has been made possible by the generosity of a number of people. Much of the information contained in this book comes from a series of interviews conducted by the author, who gratefully acknowledges the people interviewed for their enthusiasm and candour.

Interviews were conducted with:

Rodney Gooch, Manager, Central Australian Aboriginal Media Association (CAAMA) Shop, Alice Springs, who is the art co-ordinator for the Utopia artists.

Christopher Hodges, artist, gallery owner and representative for the Utopia artists.

Julia Murray, the first co-ordinator of the Utopia Batik Programme.

Jenny Green, artist and linguist, who was the first art co-ordinator for the Utopia artists.

Anne Marie Brody, Curator, The Robert Holmes à Court Collection.

Wally Caruana, Curator of Aboriginal Art, Australian National Gallery.

Mary Reid Brunstrom, co-owner, Austral Gallery, St Louis, Missouri, USA.

Special mention needs to be made of the enormous contribution that Christopher Hodges has made to the production of this book. Simply, without his assistance this project would not have been realised. I thank Helen Eager and Greg Dawes for their help, particularly with the manuscript. I would also like to thank Rossi Cole and all the staff of the CAAMA Shop, Alice Springs. Particularly, I would like to express my appreciation to Nevill Drury, Marion Day and Sue Edmonds for their production assistance. Finally, I wish to express my gratitude to Libby Slater for her inestimable contribution and support.

Michael Boulter

FOREWORD

The artists from the Utopia region live in small extended family groups, close to their important sites, maintaining strong links with traditional values. Once initiated, they paint their bodies and ceremonial objects with designs that have been handed down for generations. Since the late 1970s they have also been making images with non-traditional materials.

This new body of work was the precinct of the women until recent times, and was primarily via the batik technique. For over a decade the women developed their own distinct means of expression and facility with the medium, a fluency that has translated to new media.

Over the years, the artists have been supported by a series of art co-ordinators who have bridged the gap between this remote community and the cities, where the work is exhibited and materials can be acquired. The role of these individuals has been crucial. Rodney Gooch has fulfilled this role since 1987 and it was due to him that I became the representative of the Utopia artists. His unstinting efforts over this vital period deserve special recognition.

I first encountered the work of Utopia artists in the contemporary Australian area of the Australian National Gallery. These works on undulating silk were inspiring. I had never heard of any of the artists and only realised they were Aborigines when I read the labels.

Now, many years later, I know these artists and have much greater understanding of their culture and its relationship to their art. But looking back over the work that they made since the late 1970s, and in particular the work since 1988, it is clear to me that the most outstanding works go beyond Aboriginality. The art transcends specific cultural roots and references and thus becomes meaningful to a much wider audience.

Though many curators, critics and collectors have had difficulty in coming to terms with the art that is emerging from Aboriginal artists, let there be no mistake: this is contemporary art quite outside the realm of the tribal or the ethnographic. The media 'boom' in contemporary Aboriginal art and the folklore that surrounds it has done little to acknowledge the artistic maturity of many outstanding individuals, whose contributions are still to be recognised.

This book is a tribute to these artists.

Christopher Hodges

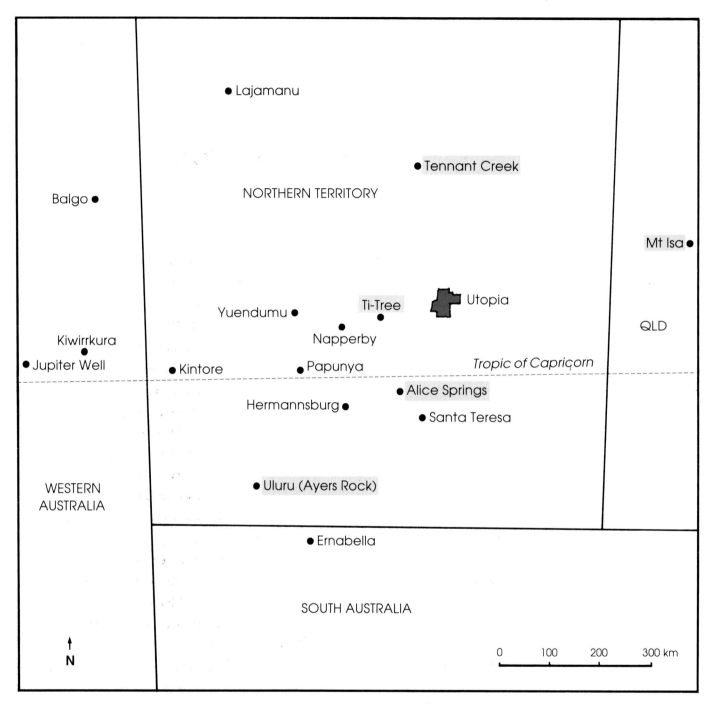

● Lajamanu

● Tennant Creek

NORTHERN TERRITORY

Balgo ●

Mt Isa ●

Utopia

Ti-Tree

Yuendumu ●

QLD

Kiwirrkura
●
● Jupiter Well

Napperby ●

Tropic of Capricorn

● Kintore

● Papunya

● Alice Springs

Hermannsburg ●

● Santa Teresa

WESTERN
AUSTRALIA

● Uluru (Ayers Rock)

● Ernabella

SOUTH AUSTRALIA

↑
N

0   100   200   300 km

The southern boundary of Utopia is approximately 270 kilometres NNE of Alice Springs. Some other Aboriginal artistic communities are noted. Major towns of the region are shaded in grey.

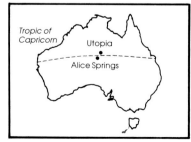

ONE

INTRODUCTION

By 8:00 am the bleach-blue sky is already forecasting a very hot day. It is windy, unusual for this hour of the morning. Having spent our first night under the stars, our first stop is Adelaide Bore to see one of the most senior artists of Utopia, Gloria Petyarre.

The trip started the day before in Alice Springs, some 270 kilometres to the south-west, at the Central Australian Aboriginal Media Association (CAAMA) Shop. The Shop's manager and art co-ordinator, Rodney Gooch, and assistant, Rossi Cole, loaded up the four-wheel drive with provisions, a mountain of primed canvases and other art materials. Also on this trip is Sydney-based artist, Christopher Hodges who, through a chance meeting four years ago became a representative for the Utopia artists.

Adelaide Bore is on the Ti-Tree Aboriginal Lease, just to the west of the Utopia Aboriginal Land; but the people here regard themselves as being part of Utopia. Centred around a windmill and a water tank on stilts, are seven houses, several outbuildings, a shed with emergency radio and another that is partly reserved for the travelling medical clinic and, on other occasions, for storing completed works of art.

Adelaide Bore is home to about 15 families. The number is never constant, as people move from outstation to outstation. If, for instance, there is a death at the outstation, people will move on; it will remain deserted for some time. This place is the site of Ronnie Price Mpetyane's kangaroo and wild plum dreamings. Ronnie Price is Gloria Petyarre's husband.

Petyarre comes out to meet the truck. This is the first time Hodges has seen Petyarre since her return from Ireland, where she and her artist sister Kathleen Petyarre accompanied the exhibition 'Utopia: A Picture Story'. The conversation turns to India, the stop-over point on the return flight to Australia. Petyarre remarks on the poverty, begging and hunger she saw; how she is glad to be home. (Hodges later comments that Petyarre is living in a state that most Westerners would regard as poverty.) There are no problems like that here, she says. The hunting has been good. The families haven't bought provisions from the Ahalpere Store on Utopia for a month, surviving instead on kangaroo, goanna and bush turkey.

Several canvases are unloaded, as well as pastels and paper for Petyarre to use. Sitting down beside the truck, on a tarpaulin to provide some protection against the ground, Hodges shows Petyarre the various techniques that can be used to achieve different effects with the pastels: using the side as well as the end of the crayon; blurring the image with a rub of the finger. The wind is blowing more strongly. Stones are used to anchor the corners. As the two talk and work, some of the other family members come and quietly look on.

Red earth scuds over the tarpaulin and paper. The decision is made to move inside the house. The tarpaulin is laid out once again on the bare concrete floor. Hodges wants to show Petyarre the methods involved in two-colour lithographic work. This requires using lithographic transfer paper and a pigment that is made into a very liquid grey opaque medium. A small child interrupts, seeking the attention Petyarre is giving to her work. Petyarre takes the interruption in her quiet, sure stride, calming the infant, whilst still carrying on her discussion with Hodges. People constantly wander in and out, take up a stance against a wall, and watch.

Petyarre studies the blank lithographic transfer paper and then dips a brush into the runny pigment. There is a constant and steady rhythm to her brushstrokes. It is evident that she has a clear vision of what she is attempting. These are the hands of an experienced artist. An artist who may only have been working with canvas for three years but has been a batik artist since the mid-1970s and has painted ceremonial body designs for most of her life.

Gooch tries his hand with the special lithographic paint and paper. Rossi Cole strums a guitar that is missing two strings. People chat and laugh whilst the artists work. After about two hours the truck is loaded up and we move on to the next outstation.

This book is an attempt to record the work to date of a group of Australian Aboriginal artists from Central Australia who live on, or nearby, some 1,800 square kilometres of land known as Utopia. With few exceptions they speak Anmatyerre and Alyawarre. They are very predominantly women.

The artists first began working in non-traditional media in the mid-1970s, when they responded enthusiastically to a series of workshops on batik. It was not until the latter stages of the 1980s that they began concentrating on works on canvas and experimenting with non-traditional sculptural forms. In recent times even parts of wrecked cars have provided the basis of celebrated expressions of their art.

The art from Utopia displays great freedom of expression, compared to the more formal work of the Pintupi and other artists of the Central and Western Desert regions. The iconography used by all these groups shows a common derivation, but works from

Utopia can range from quite figurative, to pure abstract, to more traditional depictions of Dreamings.

As the curator of Aboriginal art at the Australian National Gallery, Wally Caruana stated in an interview:

> *The artists of Utopia, and the other communities in the desert, have shown us there are a number of traditions of art in Australia. We know very much about the European ones, which have been relatively recently introduced; but what we can see now is that there are very strong traditions of art in Aboriginal Australia.*
>
> *These traditions are far from being the same across the country — take, for example, art in Arnhem Land, of the Tiwi on Bathurst and Melville Islands, the art in northern Western Australia …*[1]

To take this point further, it is frequently possible to look at a piece of artwork and identify the artist's community before recognising the particular vision and signature of an individual artist. In a census report released in 1991, some 227, 645 Australians identified themselves as being Aborigine or Torres Strait Islander, just 1.5 per cent of the population.[2] Yet, the report says, estimates of the Aboriginal population prior to white settlement are as high as one million.[3]

That a culture has successfully existed for at least 40,000 years without degrading an already harsh environment is without parallel. There must be lessons to be learnt, and art has already played an important role in increasing interest in Aboriginal cultures. White Australians, anthropologists and art historians are only just coming to terms with the realisation that Aboriginal art is the longest continuing art-form on this planet, at least twice as old as the cave paintings of Lascaux.[4] All these factors have added to the interest, mysticism and romanticism that is readily built up around any form of Aboriginal art. That the art-buying public's voracious search for the new should have finally led to the world's oldest art tradition is indeed ironic.

The artists of Utopia are relative newcomers to the Western art scene. Albert Namatjira produced his first watercolours in 1936. As Nadine Amadio says in her work on this artist:

> *… he was … one of the first Aboriginal artists to make that tremendous leap from traditional art to the art of the individual painter in a totally new medium.*
>
> *It is strange that, for example, in the Papunya Aboriginal art we are seeing today, individual artists are emerging with distinctive styles and names that are becoming nationally famous, such as Clifford Possum Tjapaltjarri, Turkey Tolson Tjupurrula and Uta Uta Tjangala amongst others. Yet, as far as one can see, they rarely sign their work.*[5]

Amadio postulates that Aboriginal artists will start to do this as values for an individual artist's work increase.

The work of the Papunya Tula artists can be traced back to 1971. It was just a few years later, in 1977, that the women of Utopia began producing batik work. Although only six years separated the two movements, it took the Utopia art advisers considerable effort to overcome the prejudiced view that their work was merely handcraft. It was many years before this same work would be lauded in the galleries of France, Germany, Ireland, Scotland and the United States.

Utopia is an area where the family clans are intent on leading as close to a traditional life as possible. Missionaries may have visited their country but no mission stations were established and their ultimate effect has been minimal. The result has been a continuous thread of traditional life — which has survived the period when Utopia was covered by a pastoral lease, as well as the inevitable incursion of Western life. Ceremonial teaching is a part of that traditional life and naturally includes painterly expression for both men and women. No matter whether the work of the Utopia artists is figurative, abstract or more traditional, it is full of meaning, born of the spirituality and traditions of the lives they lead.

It is still too early to assess the stature of the art of Utopia. However, this book is timely in being able to, first, capture the work of the leading artists whilst they are still active (the most senior of whom is in her eighties), and secondly, capture the thoughts of some of the main protagonists who have fought to see the work of these artists given due recognition and who can rejoice in the national and international acclaim the art of Utopia has already received. As Wally Caruana sees it:

> *Good art will always come to the fore. For that reason, I would think that for Utopia artists it will be a bright future.*[6]

Utopia Aboriginal Land
and sites of camps

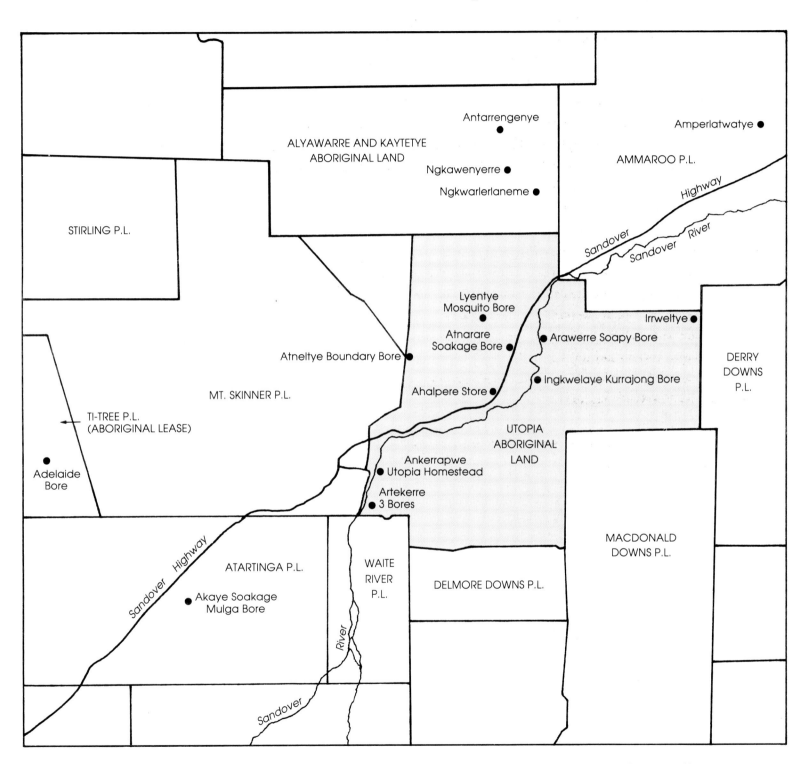

Camps are situated at bores. Where the camps are outside Utopia, they are either on other Aboriginal Lands or excisions from pastoral leases.

TWO

THE RETURN OF UTOPIA

Utopia lies across part of the traditional lands of the Anmatyerre and Alyawarre people. Anmatyerre is spoken in the southern region of Utopia and to the west, including areas such as Napperby and Coniston (scene of a massacre of Anmatyerre and Kaytetye people in 1928, following the death of a white man). The Alyawarre language is more widespread in usage, covering an area as far afield as Mt Isa in Queensland and Tennant Creek in the north.[7] Within language groups people live in family clans that are extended, complex family groupings.

The land is arid, the topography essentially flat, with the exception of rocky outcrops and small, low ranges. The climate is divided into two seasons, wet and dry. The wet season begins around October, going through until May. Although the total rainfall may be low, downpours during this time can quickly render roads impassable. The main service road to Alice Springs is the unsealed Sandover Highway which peters out some 200 kilometres east of Utopia. During an extended wet period in January 1991, Utopia (amongst other communities) made national news broadcasts when food drops from aircraft were necessary. The summers feature protracted temperatures of higher than 40°C; the winters consist mainly of warm days and freezing nights.

The Sandover River bisects Utopia. It flows only rarely — the only permanent water supplies are from bores or soakages. There is no binding pasture to hide the red soil; there is no way it could survive the extremes of climate. Rather, the landscape is dotted with kurrajong, mulga and bean wood trees and clumps of spindly, tough-leaf low scrub and spinifex. The plant life covers the earth like the thin, translucent, speckled skin of an old man. To the well-trained eye it yields a wealth of bush foods and supports a surprisingly diverse range of wildlife.

In 1979 the Anmatyerre and Alyawarre made a successful claim for the freehold title of the Utopia Pastoral Lease, thus formally returning the land from 50 years of white control to its traditional owners. The events that surround the return of the freehold cannot be underestimated. The subject of the art of Utopia is the land. It is central to every expression of the Utopia artists.

Ada Bird and Gloria Petyarre wearing
ceremonial body paint, Alice Springs,
1988

There are stark contrasts as to the notion of land ownership between non-indigenous
and Aboriginal Australians. Western belief is derived from a history of practising farming
and animal husbandry. Possession is measured in physical qualities such as boundaries.
Land is seen as a resource, viewed in terms of what is usable and what is not. Only with the
development of conservation movements have Western beliefs begun to come to terms
with the responsibilities involved with land ownership.

Artist Kathleen Petyarre gives an idea of the basis of the relationship to the land the
people of Utopia have:

> *This country really belongs to Aboriginal people. Our ancestors lived in this country, on
> this ground; the old men lived in this country, living on bush food. Aboriginal people live
> here today, looking after the country. We all look after the country, men and women
> together. The women look after their country by dancing their ceremonies. The white
> people only come lately, to this Aboriginal land.* [8]

Petyarre talks about 'belongs to' and the responsibilities involved rather than 'ownership'. This hints at the complexity of the relationship between Aborigines and the land.[9] Through the practices of sacred ceremonies and leading their lives according to the traditions and laws passed on by their ancestors, the people 'look after' their land. These laws were established during the time of the Dreaming, the time of Creation. These ancestors are still a part of the Dreamings; the Dreamings are alive and need constant renewal. Every feature of the land and the animals that walk on it is suffused with the power of a particular Dreaming.[10]

Adherence to ceremony is seen as important to the welfare of a Dreaming site. Bush tucker may flourish. The owner of the Dreaming, on seeing a fattened kangaroo the following season in the area, may remark: 'I did that.'

Ownership of a Dreaming links each individual, their clan and language group, to particular areas, sites and journeys. The journeys made by ancestors formed the topography of the landscape, the valleys, hills, rivers and soakages. It is the concept of Dreaming related to journeys that finds the greatest incompatibility with the Western notion of land possession, as journeys can encompass huge distances. Conversely, the white concept of land usage invariably involves the despoilation of land in the eyes of Aborigines and, consequently, everything sacred to the owners of the Dreamings involved.

Probably the most contentious problem has been the inability of Aboriginal people to

A group of women displaying batik at Atneltyeye (Boundary Bore), 1988

lead traditional lives when whites have claimed ownership over land. A Dreaming is a living tradition that requires a continuous lineage, otherwise it is lost. That lineage depends on ceremony and traditional life. One of the many functions of the Central Australian Aboriginal Media Association (CAAMA) has been to record old people's Dreamings (particularly those with no clear descendent) before they are lost forever.

Both women and men own Dreamings. There is 'women's business' and 'men's business'. Both are autonomous, independent and complementary; each is respected by the other.

Traditionally, men and women live separate lives. Even at the same outstation there will be a men's camp and a women's camp. As a result, the store of white understanding of each group of Aborigines has been influenced heavily by the sex of the white contact. Geoff Bardon, an art teacher, was the initiator of the Papunya Tula art movement. The painters of Papunya Tula have been predominantly male. The adult educators that started the Utopia Batik Group were female. Originally the artists of Utopia were female with only a few exceptions. The advent of a male art adviser has undoubtedly led to more men becoming involved.

The Utopia pastoral lease was first drawn up in 1927. The Aboriginal people were forced to move away from their traditional sites, nearer to homesteads where the men worked as stockhands and the women as domestics. One of the few remarkable exceptions to this delineation by sex appears to have been Emily Kame Kngwarreye, a very important person in the community and highly independent, who is now senior amongst the Utopia artists. She rode horseback in the stock camps and even in her eighties is still very strong.

The concentration of Aboriginal communities to near the station homestead continued until 1977. The mid-1970s were watershed years, following the national election in 1972 which saw the reformist Whitlam Labor Government gain power. Land Rights were given remarkable legislative priority. The Aboriginal Land Rights Commission was established under Mr Justice Woodward and it sought advice from Aboriginal and non-Aboriginal interests alike as to how the legislation should proceed. Such was the momentum created by the Land Rights movement that the Aboriginal Land Rights (Northern Territory) Act, 1976, was enacted even after the fall of the Whitlam Government a year earlier.

The period also saw the beginnings of Aboriginal legal aid services and land councils.

In 1977, the people of Utopia gained a 99 year leasehold on the Utopia Pastoral Lease, purchased through the Aboriginal Land Fund Commission. The Commission employed a white manager during the first year to provide a transition for the cattle operation. However, this proved to be unsatisfactory.

Soon after the white pastoralists left Utopia, the people began talking about moving back to their traditional country. As well as the centralised community near the station homestead at Ankerrapwe, there had been an attempt by the Northern Territory bureaucracy to create a settlement at Artekerre, three kilometres away. This settlement was to be based along the disastrous lines of Papunya and Yuendumu, where different groups from widely disparate areas had been forced together for the convenience of the white administration. Fortunately, there was not enough time before the leasehold was granted for Artekerre to grow to any size.

The outstation movement had started at Utopia well before the start of the land claim hearing that was to come in 1979. The first outstation was established at Atnarare. By having smaller land-oriented and family-based communities, the people felt the unrest and dislocation of a multi-lingual Papunya-type community could be avoided. The outstations became an important expression of the social and cultural attachment of the people to the whole of the claim area (and beyond).

The batik programme which had started in 1977 was important to the significant role the Anmatyerre and Alyawarre women played in the land claim for the Utopia Pastoral Lease. In the course of the hearing they showed how batik was able to be made in the relative isolation at the outstations, away from a central location. Batik provided a source of income and an expression of the vitality of the outstations and strength of women's life in the Utopia region.

A number of the women claimants for Utopia were also involved in the Alyawarre Kaititja [11] claim a year earlier. The knowledge they gained helped in making the women's part of the Utopia claim stronger. They were assisted by the appointment of a second female Central Land Council field worker to help them put their claim together. The information provided by Aboriginal women played a far more significant role in the claim book than at previous land claim hearings. Anthropologist Meredith Rowell recalls:

> … the women at Utopia decided to show chosen selections of their rich ceremonial life to
> the Central Land Council staff, both male and female, before the hearings, in order that
> the people organising their case would be familiar with their formidable knowledge and
> responsibilities. These displays were always an object of pride to male claimants, who
> would speak about women's business as contributing to the well-being of the country. [12]

The women prepared elaborate ceremonies, involving body designs, ceremonial objects and dances related to the claim area. In his judgement Justice Toohey recognised there was a clear demonstration of the significance their country held for them. [13]

Utopia women gave evidence about how they enjoyed creating the batiks. Julia Murray, the founding co-ordinator of the Utopia Batik Programme, brought some work to the hearing:

> At the end [of the claim hearing] I had this table of batik, and the judge and all the other
> crew were scrambling amongst it … They all bought bits of batik … [14]

Some of the women from Akaye Soakage (Mulga Bore)

Murray believed it was important for the confidence of the women as artists to see such powerful people show strong interest in their artwork.

The bulk of evidence at the hearing was presented by the men. It was still some time in the future before the role of women in traditional life was understood and given full recognition at land claim hearings. However, the Utopia claim was an important landmark in gaining this recognition. Most importantly, it was successful and the Anmatyerre and Alyawarre people were given freehold title to the pastoral lease area.

Since that time, the outstation movement has continued as more families have desired to move near to their important sites. The most recent outstation to be established was Ngkawenyerre in 1990, from a group that had been living with others at nearby Ngkwarlerlaneme. Both these camps are well outside the boundaries of the old pastoral lease. The boundaries have become irrelevant to the extent that a number of the surrounding properties have become Aboriginal lands. Where other properties are still in white hands, a number of excisions have been made.

Utopia is recognised as being a very strong, close-knit community. The governing Community Land Council consists of traditional elders who have the respect of the people in the region. This has been vital in coping with the incursion of modern white culture and technology into the region. Alcohol abuse is a major problem amongst Aboriginal communities in many areas of Australia. The Council at Utopia forbids the consumption and selling of alcohol in the region. This can be difficult to enforce at times, with an ever shifting population. However, the people have moved very decisively to stop liquor sellers.

Gooch remains firmly optimistic about the Utopia community:

> *One time I bussed everybody into town [Alice Springs]. I ended up with 120 women and children. Out of that there was only one woman who drank, and not one of them smoked cigarettes. They all spoke [their Aboriginal] language. They all lived good strong traditional lives. They seemed to be quite exceptional compared to most communities.*
>
> *Why they are stronger than everybody else, I am not sure … it is over a decade now that they have been working with these contemporary media … I have always said that if you could instil pride in Aboriginal people, you had jumped one of the biggest hurdles ever.*[15]

It is important not to gloss over the many problems that still beset communities such as Utopia, and Aboriginal people generally. However, there are many positive elements that have emerged from the experiences of the Utopia community over the past two decades, not the least being a vibrant community of artists producing their unique visions of the world and the land in which they live.

THREE

THE ART TRADITION

The population of the Utopia region is about 1,800 people. Everyone lives in small land- and family-based communities, leading as near traditional lives as possible. As part of their traditional existence people are taught ceremony. Each person, male or female, is taught their designs, how to apply them to the ground — how to cut furrows and decorate them, and how to make and decorate ceremonial instruments.

Everyone is taught as an artist from an early age. All individuals are shown how to express themselves in a strong visual manner and, importantly, how to describe their land. This tradition has gone on since time immemorial. The importance of painting has not diminished since 1788 when white occupation commenced.

As Aboriginal leader Galarrwuy Yanupingu has observed:

> *For many Australians an enduring image of their history are [sic] paintings of Captain Phillip and some soldiers raising the British Flag at Camp Cove in 1788 ... In any version ... it shows a group of strangers to our country making the first of what was to be known 190 years later as a 'land claim'.*
>
> *... When we paint — whether it is on our bodies for ceremony or on bark or canvas for the market — we are not painting for fun or profit. We are painting as we have always done to demonstrate our continuing link with our country and the rights and responsibilities we have to it. Furthermore, we paint to show the rest of the world that we own this country, and that the land owns us.[16]*

Artist Kathleen Petyarre provides a description of the structure of *Awelye*, women's ceremony, in *Utopia: A Picture Story*:

> *The old women used to [and still do] paint the ceremonial designs on their breasts, first with their fingers, and on their chests, and then with a brush called a* tyepale, *made from a stick. They painted their thighs with white paint. They painted with red and white*

ochres. Then they danced, showing their legs. The old women danced with a ceremonial stick in the earth.

The spirits of the country gave women's ceremonies to the old woman. The woman sings, then she gives that ceremony to the others, to make it strong. The old woman is the boss because the spirits of the country have given her the ceremony. So all the women get together and sing.

The old women sing these ceremonies if people are sick; they sing to heal young girls, or children. If a child is sick in the stomach, they sing. The old women are also holding their country as they dance. The old women dance with that in mind. They teach the younger women and give them the knowledge, to their granddaughters, so then all the grandmothers and granddaughters continue the tradition.[17]

The First Art Co-ordinators

The opportunity for the Utopia women to use non-traditional media came in 1977 when batik was introduced. Toly Sawenko was a white schoolteacher at Utopia at the time and was one of the first white people to take an interest in learning the culture and language of the Aboriginal communities at Utopia. A friend, Jenny Green, came out to Utopia and met the women. She ultimately became the first art co-ordinator at Utopia. Sawenko and Green formed a friendship with Cookie Pwerle, the school cook, who helped them with the language.[18]

Although the women of Utopia had hunting and ceremonial duties to perform, the mothers spent a considerable amount of time waiting each day for their children to finish school.

Green suggested to the women that while they waited they might like to learn literacy and numeracy skills and learn how to drive a vehicle. The women responded enthusiastically. Green managed to gain part-time funding for her work through the Northern Territory Education Department Adult Education scheme. She soon ended up teaching for far more than the 10 hours per week for which she was paid. She also offered to teach art and craft work, such as sewing and wood block fabric printing. Twenty to thirty women came to classes every day, their ages ranging from 13 to 75 years of age. Teaching such a divergent age group made the situation challenging: while some of the younger women had experienced schooling, the older women had not.

Green organised two craft resources women from the Institute for Aboriginal Development, Suzie Bryce and Yipati Brown, to come out to Utopia and show the women the techniques involved in making batik. Brown was a Pitjantjatjara woman from Fregon, south-west of Alice Springs. Batik had started at the Ernabella Mission many years before and had spread to Fregon, so Brown had grown up with a tradition of making batik. As she was a Pitjantjatjara woman, she did not know any Anmatyerre or Alyawarre, but was pleased to be able to successfully communicate through the batik work itself.

The first fabrics the women made were largely for their own consumption, and were turned into skirts and children's clothing. It wasn't until 1980 that the women had their first exhibition at a gallery run by Mona Byrnes in Gillen, a suburb of Alice Springs. The exhibition, a joint show of Utopia batiks and paintings by Jenny Green, proved to be a success.

Finding the money for fabrics and dyes was a constant worry. In the beginning, Green raised money by selling second-hand clothes and hot dogs on movie nights at Utopia. The Aboriginal Trust Association, funded by royalties from mining on Aboriginal lands, assisted by buying the community two utility vehicles to help cover the long distances between outstations and Alice Springs.

The first fabrics the women produced tended to imitate the patterns of commercial cloth that they saw in the stores in Alice Springs. However, the women quickly made the transition to using images from their own environment. They drew on their knowledge of plants, animals and natural forms that were important to them, and other images that until now had only been used in ceremonies.

Julia Murray, who was a Melbourne friend of Green, arrived at Utopia in 1978. She helped with the numeracy and literacy classes, but soon concentrated her efforts on batik.

Lily Sandover Kngwarreye and Emily Kame Kngwarreye with tie-dye fabrics, c. late 1970s

As Murray became more involved, Green turned to compiling a Word List of Anmatyerre, collecting oral histories, and illustrating a work on plants of the region, thus becoming less involved with day-to-day advice and support. During this time Murray applied on behalf of the women for funding from the Aboriginal Arts Board of the then Australian Council for the Arts, as well as from the Commonwealth Education Department's Aboriginal Study Grants Scheme, and thereby established the Utopia Batik Programme. These funds allowed the artists to work with silk fabric, which holds colour more strongly than cotton and is far more visually dynamic.

In the summers, when the temperatures in Central Australia become unbearably high, Murray would sell batiks in Melbourne and Sydney. She also used the trips to buy large containers of cotton T-shirts and jeans to take back to Utopia to turn into batik clothes.

The work produced was immediately identifiable and distinct from the batiks of other areas. The Ernabella batiks were very neat and immaculately executed with recognisable abstract motifs, aided by being produced in a well-established workshop. The Utopia women were far less concerned with the neatness of execution: they worked in the bush by the fire. The resultant images were very free, bold and full of life.

Murray encouraged people to experience the art form for their own pleasure and to explore it as far as they wanted:

> *I really didn't want to be saying to people who were totally fresh and who could move in any direction they wanted to … 'Well, this is good because it is neat … and this is good because it has a story. And yours, which is abstract and doesn't have a story, and doesn't have any recognisable things in it, is no good'.*[19]

Within a few years the artists became more independent in their work. The role of the art adviser developed into more one of marketing and financial administration.

Some men had asked the women to show them batiking techniques. The men's batik movement was badly stifled following the death of one of the senior batik men. They were already inhibited by being involved in an activity regarded as 'women's business' and therefore separate from men. There were also cultural problems in dealing with a female art co-ordinator. Since the introduction of work on canvas and a male art co-ordinator, many more men have produced non-traditional artwork.

Batik, which started as women's business was now essentially entrenched as women's business.

Following the success of the Alice Springs show in 1980, the next major exhibition of batik was 'Floating Forests of Silk: Utopia Batik from the Desert' at the Adelaide Festival Centre in 1981. Silver Harris, who was the exhibition co-ordinator, had heard of the work and came to visit the artists at Utopia. She was very excited by what she saw. Through a grant from the Aboriginal Arts Board, 12 artists, including Emily Kame Kngwarreye,

Dorothy and Patsy Kemarre, Lucky Kngwarreye and Rosemary and Joy Petyarre, travelled on the Ghan train to Adelaide, accompanied by Green and Murray. It was the first time any of the artists had travelled interstate. Green and Murray took spinifex with them and decorated the exhibition space to evoke the desert. The show gained considerable media interest, with Murray doing both television and radio interviews.

With assistance from the Department of Aboriginal Affairs, the Aboriginal Development Commission, as well as the Aboriginal Arts Board, Utopia batik was able to be exhibited throughout the country at events such as Craft Council shows and at a black cultural festival staged as part of the black protest against the Brisbane Commonwealth Games.

Murray showed great determination and belief in the quality of the batiks as art. She showed pieces to the Museum of Victoria and the yet to be opened Australian National Gallery. Both institutions acquired works.

Women from the Utopia Batik Group prepare to board 'The Ghan' en route to the Adelaide Festival in 1980

I had an appointment with the buyer from the Australian National Gallery. There was this really incongruous scene in the foyer of the Melbourne Hilton: me with my red-dirt covered bag and the buyer in his suit kneeling on the floor, looking at these amazingly colourful batiks all over the floor.[20]

In 1981 Murray applied for a grant on behalf of the Utopia artists under the Queen Elizabeth II Silver Jubilee Trust Award for Young Australians. The grant enabled three women to see batik techniques and production in their traditional environment in Indonesia: Nora, Rosemary and Joy Petyarre, accompanied by Murray. Selection of the artists was narrowed down to those brave enough to travel on a plane. When the women arrived in Indonesia they were shocked by the begging they saw. They had come from a very insulated, nomadic, extended family environment.

They spent some time having technical training before returning without delay. The trip left a deep impression and provided some fantastic stories for around the camp-fire at night.

After five years, Murray reached a point where she felt that there was little more that she could offer the artists:

> I thought the batik was beautiful in its own right and that eventually people would appreciate it, but it was probably naive ... I should have gone the canvas way, in terms of the struggle with people not seeing it as artwork, rather as a relatively expensive piece of material.[21]

Murray was replaced by Deborah Speedy, who was in turn followed by Bonita Liddle, Helga Muschinski, Cathy Barnes and eventually Rodney Gooch as the representative of the Central Australian Aboriginal Media Association (CAAMA). Green points to the importance of Speedy and Barnes, who remained for a number of years and succeeded in having Utopia work exhibited throughout the country (for details, see the Exhibition List on p.174). Barnes was also a seamstress and her input in this area was very much valued.

The role of the art co-ordinators was vital and continues to be so. There would be no contemporary art from Utopia without the women who established the batik programme, gained funds to provide the materials, and marketed the work. Rodney Gooch and CAAMA have provided an even more sophisticated art representation, that has enabled the work of the artists to survive and now flourish without any financial support.

RODNEY GOOCH AND CAAMA

Rodney Gooch arrived in Alice Springs in the late 1970s en route to Afghanistan, but did not become involved with CAAMA until 1982. In between time he learnt about camels from an old Afghan camel driver and became the first person to walk a camel train from Alice Springs to the east coast of Australia, finishing the journey at Byron Bay.

He returned to Alice Springs with the intention of putting together another camel train

Showing 'The Utopia Suite' wood block prints to the women artists at Akaye Soakage, October 1990

and heading west. In the 18 months that followed he worked in various jobs trying to save enough money. During this time he came to realise how appallingly the Aboriginal people of the region were treated.

In response, he began running socials for Aboriginal people, featuring bands from the bush.

This led to a short-term job offer in 1982 with CAAMA, recording, distributing and selling cassettes of contemporary Aboriginal music. His efforts were so successful that eventually he helped to set up a recording studio. Through visiting communities throughout the Central and Western Deserts, he realised there was an urgent need to record sacred Aboriginal material, as many of the people were old and the music might be lost with their deaths.

In 1983 Gooch set up a CAAMA shop in a converted generator shed on the outskirts of Alice Springs. The product range consisted of six albums on cassette. However, word spread that an Aboriginal outlet run by an Aboriginal organisation had opened. Paintings and coolamons made by local artists soon started appearing on the walls and shelves.

In 1987 Gooch was approached by the Department of Aboriginal Affairs to represent the Utopia Women's Batik Group (as they were then called). There was an offer to support the representation with funding, but the money never eventuated.

He met with some 20 of the artists 'who produced lengths of silk batik in colours and designs that appeared to dance in the sun as they were proudly unfurled'.[22] As he quickly discovered: 'They were a group of people who were receptive to whatever you did, and really enjoying doing the work for the pleasure of it'.[23]

Gooch wanted to have a clearer idea of the work of the individual artists and felt the group had been lacking direction and structure. Thus he initiated the survey of the stories of each artist that has become known as 'A Picture Story'. Made up of 88 batik silks of roughly the same size (2.4 x 1.2 metres), the survey was produced between January and March, 1988 and each artist was paid the same amount of money for their work.

'A Picture Story' was used to open the first Aboriginal cultural institute, the Tandanya Centre in Adelaide, in October 1989, and has subsequently been exhibited in Ireland. The survey has become a major cultural document for the people of the region and has served to further strengthen the unity of the artists.

Yet whilst they were continuing to produce magnificent work, Gooch was frustrated by the restrictions of exhibiting them through the 'craft' network of shows and displays. Gallery rooms, designed for handicrafts with ceiling heights often only 2.5 metres, made it impossible to properly hang batiks that averaged two metres high. Gooch was determined to pursue 'arts' venues with higher ceilings which would at least give the batiks a reasonable chance to be shown at their best.

In 1988, about a year after Gooch took over representation, a chance meeting took place between Sydney-based artist, Christopher Hodges, and a representative of CAAMA, Connie Craige. Craige was in Sydney, following a show in Canberra. Hodges, who had previously seen Utopia work in the Australian National Gallery, met Craige at a dinner:

> *I asked her if she had any works with her and she produced from her bag some absolutely outstanding pieces of silk batik … As soon as I saw them I thought my friends would be very interested in them. So the next day I sold every one of them.*[24]

Craige arrived back in Alice Springs with no batiks and as yet no money. Gooch was horrified. Sure that the batiks were lost, he was surprised when the money from Hodges soon arrived in Alice Springs. Hodges' success led to another exhibition at his studio home. After using hired spaces for a short while, he opened Utopia Art Sydney, at the beginning of 1989.

THE ROBERT HOLMES à COURT COLLECTION

Appointed a representative of the artists, Hodges was able to show important works to museums and major collectors. 'A Picture Story' had been devised as one collective work and it was vital that the survey be kept together. Hodges showed the batiks to Anne Brody,

Rodney Gooch collecting finished batik from women at Atneltyeye (Boundary Bore), 1988

the curator of The Robert Holmes à Court Collection. Her positive response was matched by the desire of the Holmes à Courts to acquire complete collections which had significance beyond the individual works. One of the Collection's first Aboriginal art acquisitions had been the landmark 'Mr Sandman' collection of 27 paintings by Papunya Tula artists in 1981.

The Robert Holmes à Court Collection purchased the survey and has gone on to acquire other Utopia surveys: 'A Summer Project', the first group survey of works on canvas, and a watercolour collection. Brody is strongly supportive of the surveys:

> *It is not like you are dealing with a history of art … [where] everyone knows all the works that were painted … and people tend to work backwards in discovering things. By having these three collections … right at the beginning, it is just the reverse. You are able to see how people go forward.* [25]

The Robert Holmes à Court Collection has played an important role in the promotion of Aboriginal art in general. The Collection started buying in 1980, a long time before some major art galleries in Australia began collecting contemporary Aboriginal art.

Certainly the purchase of some one thousand works has provided the market with a level of confidence that it may well not have achieved in the Collection's absence. Even though it is private, the Collection operates like a public gallery. The Holmes à Court family has been a generous lender, both nationally and internationally.

As well, The Robert Holmes à Court Foundation has funded the CAAMA/Utopia Artist-in-Residence project to build up a store of works by individual artists. In 1990 the two recipients were Emily Kame Kngwarreye and Louie Pwerle.

THE MOVE TO OTHER MEDIA

In 1988 Gooch and Hodges, accompanied by senior Papunya artist, Clifford Possum Tjapaltjarri, took the 'Time Before Time' exhibition to St Louis, Missouri. This compilation show featured Utopia batiks, some paintings by Utopia men and works by Western Desert artists.

Gooch endeavoured to show batiks to a number of United States museums, but the constant reply was 'no craft please'. After discussion with Hodges, Gooch decided to organise an experimental survey amongst the Utopia artists to see if they would like to try acrylic painting.

The survey was completed over the summer of 1988–89. Everyone was offered the same size canvas (approximately 60 x 90 centimetres) and given the four basic colours Aboriginal artists have always used: black, red ochre, yellow ochre and white. Tjapaltjarri suggested the canvases be primed grey. One hundred canvases were handed out and eventually 81 returned. This survey became known as 'A Summer Project'. It was later acquired by The Robert Holmes à Court Collection,

The association with Rodney Gooch and CAAMA has led the artists into a wide range of new media — to canvas (and with it, the emergence of a school of male artists), sculpture (which has also involved a number of men), watercolour, wood block printing, screenprinting and works in mixed media.

Within the artist community there appears to have developed a number of specialisations. Ngkwarlerlaneme, and latterly Ngkawenyerre, primarily produce sculpture. The artists of Antarrengenye have developed a neo-Western form of landscape with flattened perspectives. The women of Ingkwelaye are producing highly decorative work.

The opportunity to work in such a wide range of media has been due to the direct involvement of Rodney Gooch, in association with Christopher Hodges and fellow artist Helen Eager. Hodges and Eager have both been art teachers and are skilled in different media. They have been able to pass on their skills to the artists with great success, particularly in wood block printing and screenprints.

Undoubtedly, a number of artists have begun to emerge with important individual visions and expression. There appears to be almost universal agreement within the Australian art scene that the future of contemporary Aboriginal art will focus more on individual artists. This is as much a part of the education of the marketplace as any other factor. As Hodges sees it:

> *The art community has been exposed to this beast called 'Aboriginal art' and Australia has any number of Aboriginal communities, plus urban Aboriginal people. Within any one of those communities, and Utopia is no exception, there are any number of artists who have something worthwhile to say as individuals.*
>
> *No-one has a problem telling a Jackson Pollock from a Willem de Kooning ... because we have studied, applied discernment — we have educated ourselves.*
>
> *Yet when people at the moment are confronted by a broad mass of Aboriginal paintings, they aren't looking for those same signs, even though they exist. But that will change.*[26]

Evidence tends to support this view. Over the past two years Emily Kame Kngwarreye, Louie Pwerle, Ada Bird Petyarre, Lyndsay Bird Mpetyane and Gloria Petyarre have all held successful solo shows.

FOUR

THE BATIKS

Batik was the first non-traditional art-form introduced at Utopia and remains the cornerstone of Utopia art, even since the emergence of other art-forms.

The batiks are made by using a *tjanting* and brushes to apply hot wax, in this instance, to silk fabric. The *tjanting* is a Javanese invention that has a handle, a small bowl which holds melted wax, and a capillary spout down which the wax flows. The design is 'painted' onto the fabric with the *tjanting* or a brush. The fabric is then dyed. This process can be repeated a number of times, using different coloured dyes. Batik involves a reduction technique, where the area available to work on is reduced with each step. Brushes are normally used to cover large areas with wax. The *tjanting* is used for more detailed work.

Ada Bird Petyarre using a tjanting to apply wax to a batik, 1990

Batiking at Ingkwelaye (Kurrajong Bore) using baby's baths and drying on the stockyard fence, c. 1980

The application of wax needs to be sufficient to saturate the fabric, so as the image can be clearly seen through the reverse. Dyeing is done in sequence from lightest to darkest shades. Once the artist has completed 'painting' and dyeing, the wax is boiled out and the fabric hung up to dry.

Batik is not indigenous to Australia. The nearest country to Australia with a strong batik tradition is Indonesia, where two forms exist: stencilled and hand-drawn. Undoubtedly the production of stencilled batiks has undermined the perceived artistic value of hand-drawn batik worldwide, a prejudice that has made the promotion of the batik work of the artists of Utopia difficult.

A reasonably quick but close examination of a hand-drawn batik will reveal the individual hand and vision, the composition without repetition. Add to these attributes the special qualities of the silk — the sensuous movement and touch, the sense of life created by the merest zephyr, the veined texture where the wax has cracked before the dyeing process — and it is possible to understand why there has been a dramatic increase in batik as an art-form.

Julia Murray describes the batiks of the first exhibition at Gillen[27] as 'really stunning … they were wild and free. They were abstract and free-form'[28]. The uninhibited, unencumbered vivacity of the batik work has continued unabated. Anne Brody, Curator of The Robert Holmes à Court Collection, recalls her first sighting of the 88 silks that make up 'A Picture Story':

'It was just one amazing, exciting image after another. It was something that excited me more than anything that I had seen in a long time, precisely because it was so different and contrary to my expectations.[29]'

In *Utopia: A Picture Story*, which is about this collection, she states:

> *As one might expect, given that* A Picture Story *represents such a large cross-section of work from a specific period, not all the images it contains are 'great art'. Some works are in fact first attempts to produce something different whilst other are 'masterpieces' by any definition.* [30]

The opening show in the Main Exhibition Hall of the Tandanya Aboriginal Cultural Institute, Adelaide, in October 1989, was an overwhelming sight. The building was an heritage-listed former power station allowing the hall to be 80 metres long with 10 metre high ceilings. Each of the eight-one 2.4 x 1.2 metre batiks of 'A Picture Story' was hung in panels of flowing silk around the walls. The works have subsequently been shown at the Royal Hibernian Academy, Dublin.

In 1988, the batik artists followed 'A Picture Story' with a series of monumental scale works, up to 6 x 2.5 metres, which showed their ease at working with the medium and the ability to adapt to such a large scale.

THE PLATES

Gloria Petyarre's *Awelye* (Plate 1) is roughly one metre square and has swirling radiating lines that depict, in the abstract, women wearing body paint designs. The wax has been applied in a manner not unlike the application of body paint in ceremony.

Emily Kame Kngwarreye's brown and white batik (Plate 2) is typical of her work in 1988, with very direct application of wax and the use of only one dye. The plant motifs are similar to her body paint designs. Quite a number of her pieces from this time drew on the same inspiration.

Rosemary Petyarre, in her untitled work (Plate 3) has created a swirling image of linear patterns derived from native grasses. Lena Pwerle's striking yellow and red design on a black background (Plate 4) shows a consummate use of colour to make a potent abstract image.

The floral batik of Ruby Kngwarreye (Plate 5) is indicative of quite a lot of work pertaining to the period prior to 'A Picture Story' which was more design-oriented. Around the edges are triangles that represent rocks. After 'A Picture Story', most artists concentrated on depicting stories.

Mavis Holmes Petyarre's work (Plate 6) relates to the images she used on the car door (see Plate 57) and the big painted landscapes which came later. Here she painted special places that have significance for her, but she depicted them in a neo-Western, naive style.

Edie Kemarre's batik (Plate 7) has structured abstracted Dreaming designs that in the work's purity give no indication of its Aboriginal derivation.

Mavis Petyarre's batik (Plate 8) comes from 'A Picture Story'. There is imagery that is readily translatable. The arrows are the footprints of pigeons, which become 'U' shapes representing people sitting around a site. The women's body paint design depicted at the top shows breasts and the paint for the shoulders and chest. The circle in the middle is painted around the navel. There is a dual image with other women sitting at the ceremony.

Lyndsay Bird Mpetyane's piece (Plate 9) depicts men's ceremony. There is a central site with people gathered around, and smaller sites with others gathered around them. The combination of linear elements makes this a most dynamic composition, focusing on the central roundel.

Julie Purvis Mpetyane's work (Plate 10) also comes from 'A Picture Story' and has quite literal depictions of ancestral women in body paint designs and headdress, travelling to the Bush Potato site. They are watching food cooking in a pit, whilst other animals gather. The strength of the work relies on the strong draftsmanship used to describe the organic nature of the forms.

Plate 1
Gloria Petyarre *Awelye* 1989

Plate 2
Emily Kame Kngwarreye *Untitled* 1988

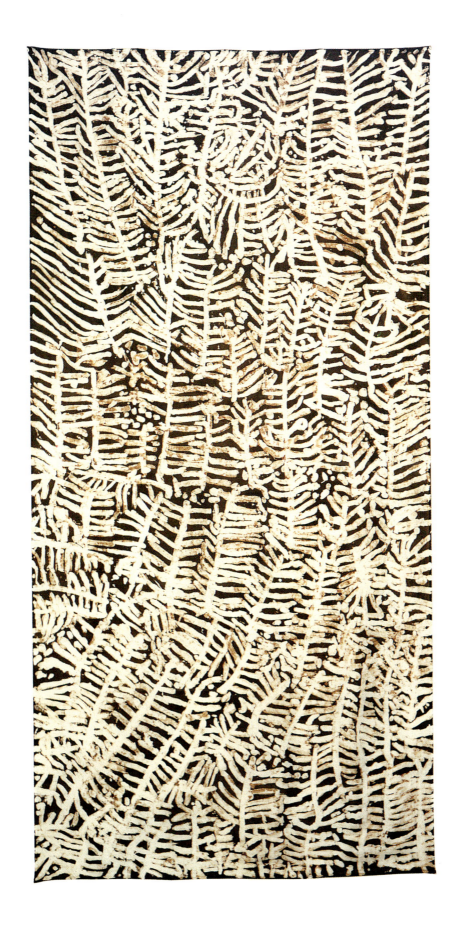

Plate 3
Rosemary Petyarre *Untitled* 1990

Plate 4
Lena Pwerle *Untitled* 1990

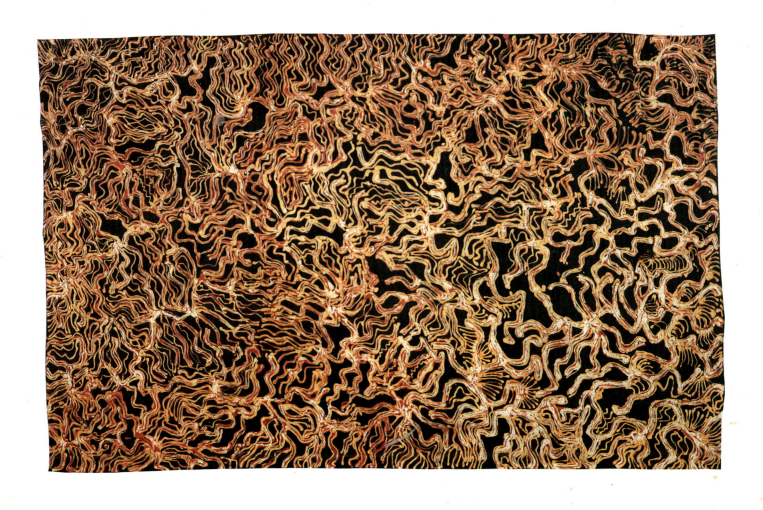

Plate 5
Ruby Kngwarreye *Untitled* 1988

Plate 6
Mavis Holmes Petyarre *Untitled* 1989

Plate 7
Edie Kemarre *Untitled* 1988

Plate 8
Mavis Petyarre *Flock Pigeon Dreaming*

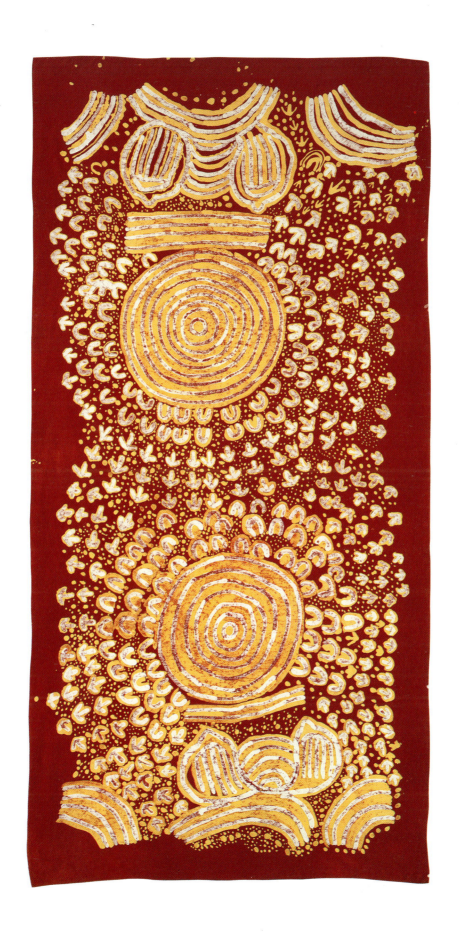

Plate 9
Lyndsay Bird Mpetyane *Men's Ceremony* 1988

Plate 10
Julie Purvis Mpetyane *Bush Potato Dreaming*

FIVE

THE CANVASES

The first significant works on canvas at Utopia were done by the men. When Gooch was organising the batik survey, 'A Picture Story', Lyndsay Bird Mpetyane and Colin Bird Mpetyane approached him to ask if they could work on canvas. The paintings that they produced were very strong and traditional. Lyndsay's work, in particular, displayed enormous promise.

When Gooch and Hodges were compiling the 'Time Before Time' exhibition to be shown in the United States, several of Lyndsay's paintings were included. The major work of the exhibition was a six panel piece called *Ilbanda* (see Plate 34), the Bush Plum Dreaming, painted by its custodians, Paddy Jungala, Engarlarka and Lyndsay Bird Mpetyane. This work now hangs in the St Louis Opera House in Missouri.

The summer of 1988–89 marked the first major project on canvas with the survey, 'A Summer Project'. Once the decision was made to conduct the survey,[31] considerable logistics were involved in supplying the artists with materials. Uncertain of the exact number who would want to participate, Gooch and Hodges decided that 100 canvases should be made.

Gooch and Hodges also agreed to use the finest quality materials, even though this would be the first attempt by nearly all the artists to work in the medium. The rationale was 'if lesser quality materials were used and the paintings turned out fantastic, we would regret it forever'[32]. Belgian linen was chosen, as well as top-grade Chromacryl acrylic paint. The wood was Pacific Maple, chamfered as in gallery frames to ensure the canvas surface did not touch the wood.

The choice of acrylic (synthetic polymer) paint was automatic. The artists work out in the open. Red earth is carried in every breeze — it would be impossible for oils to dry before being corrupted by dirt.

The CAAMA four-wheel-drive truck was loaded with primed canvases, brushes and paint, and the materials delivered to the seven outstations where artists were participating. The interchange that followed mirrors the regular events of today. Within two weeks, artists visiting Alice Springs dropped in completed works at the CAAMA Shop. Gooch

Emily Kame Kngwarreye having just completed an exhausting recording of her ceremonial music

returned to Utopia a further two weeks later and picked up the bulk of the canvases. Still others continued to filter into the CAAMA Shop for some time afterwards.

The 81 canvases that eventually formed 'A Summer Project' make up a remarkable record of the transition of well-established artists to a new medium. The images not only reflected previous batik work, but included many that were completely fresh — they had no precedent in imagery or style.

As with all surveys, particular works stood out. Emily Kame Kngwarreye's canvas, *Emu Woman* (Plate 11) showed the artist's instant affinity with the medium; where even her temperament was better suited to the immediacy of acrylic (compared to the lengthier processes of batik). The canvas showed the trademark of her work in batik: a layer of linear patterns and bold dotting derived from body paint designs.

Kngwarreye made clear her preference for acrylic. Most of the others involved in 'A Summer Project' responded enthusiastically to continuing work in the medium.

By the following summer it was felt that tradition should be followed: another survey was conducted. A set of rectangular works, 45 x 30 centimetres, and another of oval boards, approximately 90 x 60 centimetres at the widest points, were produced in an attempt to record all the body paint designs of the community. This also fulfilled the on-going CAAMA objective 'to support and encourage cultural traditions'.

The oval shape was chosen to reflect the many traditional objects made in this form — coolamons, shields and dancing boards. Again the response produced the unexpected: some of the artists interpreted the body paint designs, usually shown as just an abstraction, in a far more literal manner with striking images of the designs on people.

From each of these two surveys came on-going developments. An immediate example was the series of paintings that formed the backdrop to a sculptural show called 'The Figure'[33]. The paintings were developed directly from the ovals.

Acrylic brought with it a number of important technical advantages inherent in the medium, particularly when compared with batik. Batik is a one-hit medium. If you miss, the whole work is ruined. With acrylic the artists can paint out areas or change colours if they wish to make revisions. Because acrylic entails building layers (the opposite of the reduction technique of batik where each stage reduces the workable area), there is greater room for experimentation.

The leading artists have quickly mastered the manipulative possibilities and have been able to greatly expand their vocabulary of markings. Not only has the range of colours significantly increased, but the artists can also adjust the tonal range with far greater sensitivity. This can be particularly seen in Gloria Petyarre's work where she uses close tonal values in different colours, creating a dynamic optical intensity. Her work features powerful structural linear patterns derived from body painting, outlined with single dots (see Plate 18). At other times the structural pattern becomes submerged in a sea of dots, the tonal relationships causing the structure to dissolve into the fabric of the design (see Plate 17).

An interesting comparison can be made between the work of Gloria Petyarre and her sister Ada Bird Petyarre. Though they paint the same stories, and similarities can be perceived in the overall design structures of their work, their styles are distinct.

Gloria Petyarre with her grandson

60

Lyndsay Bird Mpetyane with his painting 'Snake Dreaming' at Akaye Soakage (Mulga Bore), October 1990

Ada Bird Petyarre uses sinuous, flowing bands as the dominant forms, often to the exclusion of any form of dotting (see Plate 14). Throughout the body of her work the bands have been explored not only as a subject (as a technique of depicting her Dreamings), but also as a painterly mark. Some works feature watery bands, others workings with her fingers. She also uses solid bands of varying colours to set up a rhythmic field, providing a current through the picture. Yet another distinctive element to her work is her technique of drawing with dots.

Emily Kame Kngwarreye's latest work uses layer upon layer of coloured dots, dabs and lines of very minutely varying hues. This would be technically impossible with batik. Her painting started with specific subjects that depicted designs from body paint images or Dreaming maps showing important sites. Now her paintings have a different vision. With the assistance of Kathleen Petyarre translating, Kngwarreye was asked to explain the stories to her paintings. She replied:

> *Whole lot, that's whole lot, Awelye (my Dreaming), Arlatyeye (pencil yam), Arkerrthe (mountain devil lizard), Ntange (grass seed), Tingu (a Dreamtime pup), Ankerre (emu), Intekwe (a favourite food of emus, a small plant), Atnwerle (green bean), and Kame (yame seed). That's what I paint: whole lot.[34]*

Thus she appears to have moved from specific subjects to an abstraction of her complete world. It is therefore not surprising that her most recent work has an overall field quality, not unlike Western Abstract Expressionists such as Jackson Pollock or Ralph Balson. Even in a Western sense, Kngwarreye has gone beyond her cultural roots.

Since the appointment of a male art adviser, Rodney Gooch, in 1987, and particularly since the introduction of the acrylic medium, an increasing number of men have become involved: Louie Pwerle, Paddy Ngale, Paddy Petyarre, Billy Petyarre, Wally Petyarre, as well as Lyndsay Bird Mpetyane and others.

Men's painting differs significantly from that painted by the women. The paintings of men are more iconic and less descriptive than those of women. The visual symbols significant to men have traditionally been based on the concentric circle with parallel lines emerging. Further descriptive elements may be used in the paintings. Though this narrow basis of subject could easily lead to repetition, the men have shown great inventiveness in their still disciplined approach.

This has certainly proved to be the case with Lyndsay Bird Petyarre. Like all of the leading artists he has shown a consistent innovative ability, using the subject of his work to experiment with various technical possibilities. The results have ranged from the very bold to remarkably sensitive and subtle expressions.

Two of the communities of Utopia have evolved their own distinct styles of neo-Western images. The Antarrengenye artists first developed a landscape tradition (alongside more traditional expression) when working with batik. Their large-scale canvases show sites in a style similar to the Namatjira school. Important places are shown using a Western manner — in some works animal tracks, water-holes and caves can be seen — however, they are still linked to traditional stories and places (see Plate 31).

The Ngkwarlerlaneme group which moved to Ngkawenyerre often showed composite images of foliage, footprints, tracks and animal life in their batik. This has become more intensified since the group began painting. The canvases are filled with detail: they are descriptive, but within them are a great many narratives of daily life and Dreamings, as with Audrey Kngwarreye's *Camp Scene* (see Plate 24).

The move to acrylic and canvas has greatly increased the profile of the Utopia artists, both in Central Australia and within the general art scene in Australia. While the whole group exhibits a high level of artistic ability, the strength of individual artists continues to emerge.

At the time of writing there has only been one retrospective of an individual contemporary Aboriginal artist, Clifford Possum Tjapaltjarri, even though he has a number of peers whose work can be traced back 20 years. The Clifford Possum retrospective was held in London in 1988, and has yet to be seen in Australia. The Tandanya Centre in Adelaide has held a retrospective that combined the works of six artists. This situation will continue until the perceived need to approach contemporary

Aboriginal art from a separate and possibly tribal-based standpoint is diminished.[35]

The artists of Utopia have a particular and very special background. However, they have developed and reacted in a manner that is directly comparable to groups of Western artists. Fortunately, the move to more solo shows continues apace and, with such a transition, a growing appreciation of the individual visions of contemporary Aboriginal artists will quickly follow.

THE PLATES

Emily Kame Kngwarreye has become the pre-eminent artist of the Utopia group with the transition to work on canvas. The three works clearly show the full range of her styles. *Emu Woman* (Plate 11) shows her typical trademarks: a layer of linear pattern covered with a layer of dotting, both elements of which are derived from body paint designs. In Plate 12, the work is based on a map almost completely covered by a layer of dots which overlay the work below. In *Intekwe (Pareke)* (Plate 13) the linear work is completely missing. This major canvas depicts the favourite seeds of the emu. Highly atmospheric, the field of dots evokes a strong desert mood.

Ada Bird Petyarre has used lines with a very limited palette in *Bush Yam Awelye* (Plate 14), in a similar manner to her batik work. The painting is notable for the power and complexity that has been derived from such simple elements. *Ntange Awelye* (Plate 15) is Ada Bird Petyarre's first work on canvas and forms part of 'A Summer Project'. Here the body paint designs are clear and bold. The women are meeting in ceremony in the middle. The work again shows the importance of line in her work.

Gloria Petyarre's *Awelye* (Plate 16) also deals with body paint designs. The paint almost appears to have been applied by the finger, much as is the case when it is physically applied to the body. Her untitled work (Plate 17) shows the same body paint designs but they have been transformed into a completely abstract image. The body design provides the structure, the layers of colour and close tonal values energise the field. With much less 'dotting' *Sacred Grasses* (Plate 18) uses a strong linear pattern to anchor the design.

Kathleen Petyarre is also a sister of Gloria and Ada. *Ankerrthe Awelye* (Plate 19) is a prime example of the rhythmic dotted-linear pattern. The painting depicts clusters of women with bowls and digging sticks in the corner and centre.

Each of the three sisters has used the same iconography, yet has managed to provide a personal and individual interpretation.

In the three examples of Lyndsay Bird Mpetyane's work (Plates 20–22), the artist displays his virtuosity and willingness to explore the acrylic medium. He has never limited himself to repeating images, though his 'signature' is identifiable and recognisable throughout. In *Mulga Apple Dreaming* (Plate 20), the use of pure lines without any dots was a theme that he explored throughout 1990. *Ceremony* (Plate 21) was produced in early 1989, whilst *Wild Bee Dreaming* (Plate 22) came from later that year. The move to the abstracted image can be seen as a logical progression from his early iconographic works. Whilst it is not immediately apparent, Mpetyane uses quite a deal of underpainting. *Wild Bee Dreaming* features several different base colours that are used discreetly underneath the composition to affect the colour combinations above.

Louie Pwerle's *Altyerre* (Plate 23) is derived from ground painting, as well as body designs. The infill dotting has been relegated to a very secondary role by the strong iconic motifs that are typical of his work.

Audrey Kngwarreye is a leading artist from the Ngkawenyerre group, which is noted for its depictions of camp scenes. This painting (Plate 24) has a mountain range, clouds and a rainbow represented in very Western manner. However, the vegetation does not change in scale from the foreground to the background. There are no elements overlapping. The picture contains many happy scenes of hunting and gathering but, larger than life and looming over everything else, is a python and a smaller snake. Also well out of scale are a series of witchetty grubs and bushflowers.

Ronnie Price is the husband of Gloria Petyarre. This painting (Plate 25) comes from the Body Paint Design Collection and shows again the iconography at the core of Utopia men's work. There is no reliance on dotting. It is a simple powerful statement of traditional images. Compare this to Ada Bird Petyarre's piece from the same series (Plate 26), where she has turned the traditional to her own interpretation. The woman is dressed for ceremony, with a cockatoo headdress and body paint designs on the figure itself, which

Engarlaka, Paddy Jungala, Lyndsay Bird Mpetyane and Paddy Ngale with 'Ilbanda' which now hangs in the St Louis Opera House, Missouri

64

was highly innovative at the time. The third work from the Collection (Plate 27) is by June Bird Petyarre. This shows breasts with body paint design on them at the top of the painting. The rest of the work employs a very contemporary use of closely aligned dot technique. The central roundel is the ceremonial design for the belly. The cluster of 'U' shapes at the bottom are women gathered around ceremonial ground designs.

Bush Flowers by Ally Kemarre (Plate 28) uses a floral motif to create a strong composition. The dashes of background colour take this painting a long way from traditional images, yet the subject matter is firmly a part of traditional Aboriginal life.

Tammy Petyarre is one of the younger artists at Utopia and shows a correspondingly youthful and vibrant use of colour in *Bush Tobacco* (Plate 29). The bright paints came from a shopping expedition to the Alice Springs K-Mart supermarket. This image is very contemporary, with a little relationship to any traditional expression.

Lena Pwerle's *Snake and Honey Ant* (Plate 30) is one of her earlier paintings. Throughout her work she has been consistently concerned with figures within a ground. The figures are all visible but are surrounded by a modulating or mottling layer of dots. The choice of vibrant pinks in this work is evidence of her early experimentation. The dividing snake gives a sense of time and change.

The combined work of Mavis Holmes Petyarre and May Baily Petyarre (Plate 31) is a vast landscape of sites near Antarrengenye. Depicted are hills, waterholes and special caves near to where the artists live. The work is notable for its working of colours to create a brooding, stormy sky and a landscape of hidden but latent energy.

Violet Petyarre's *Ngangkare* (Plate 32) is from the rectangular Small Board Collection produced at the same time as the ovals. An abstraction of body designs, it is a prime example of the tensions and dynamics that can be created within a limited range of colour and design.

Eileen Kngwarreye's work *Kwertatye* (plate 33) is also from the same series. Here the artist has chosen to show the body paint designs on the fearsome ritual law enforcer. The *kwertatye* exists on a number of levels: as an ancestral spirit; in ceremony where a person acts out the role of the *kwertatye*, and the person who is the law enforcer within a community. The body paint has been applied using an unusual technique that blurs the distinction between dots and lines. This reflects the plant matter that is used in making the marks on the body in this instance.

The six panel *Ilbanda* (plate 34) is the work of three male artists who are the custodians of the Dreaming, and clearly shows the importance of concentric circle iconography in men's painting. There is still great freedom of interpretation: each panel shows the distinction that can be drawn between the iconography of the Utopia men and the grid-like circles and lines of the *tingari* of the Western Desert painters.

Plate 11
Emily Kame Kngwarreye *Emu Woman* 1988–1989

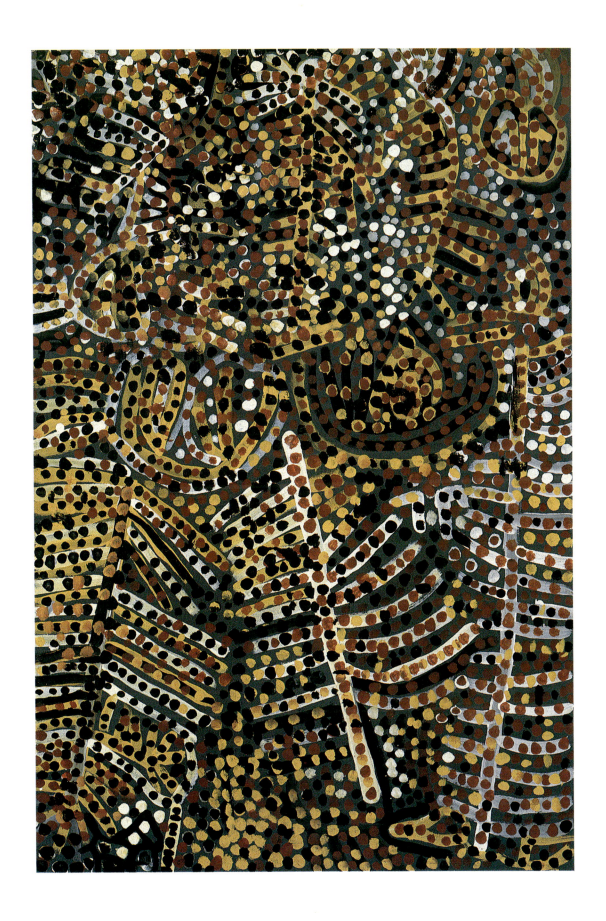

Plate 12
Emily Kame Kngwarreye *Untitled* 1990

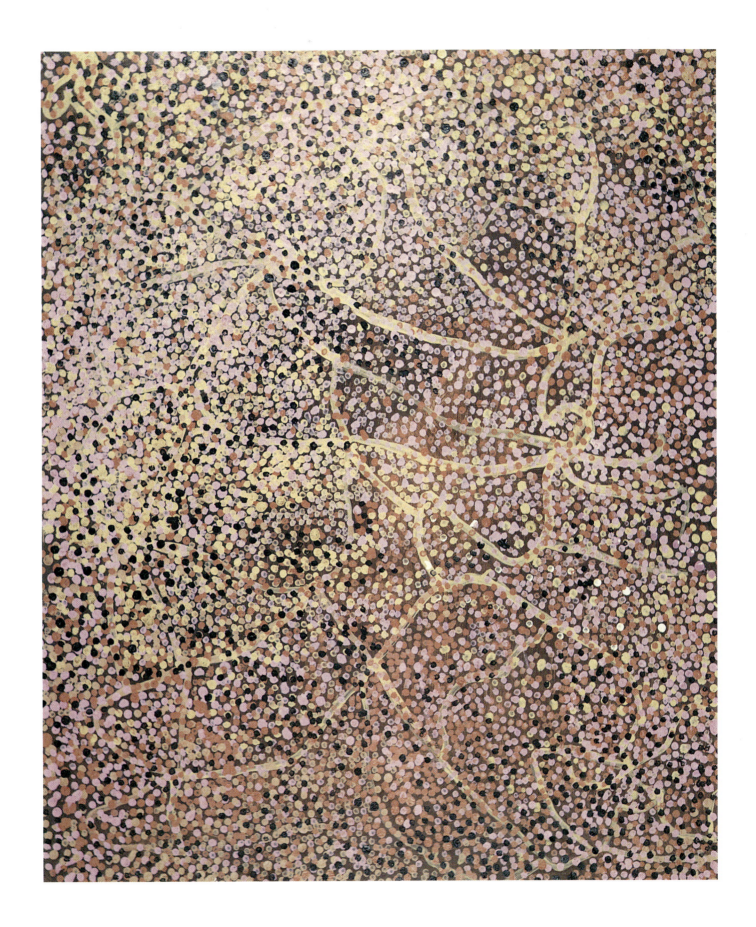

Plate 13
Emily Kame Kngwarreye *Intekwe (Pareke)* 1990

Plate 14
Ada Bird Petyarre *Bush Yam Awelye* 1990

Plate 15
Ada Bird Petyarre *Ntange Awelye* 1988–89

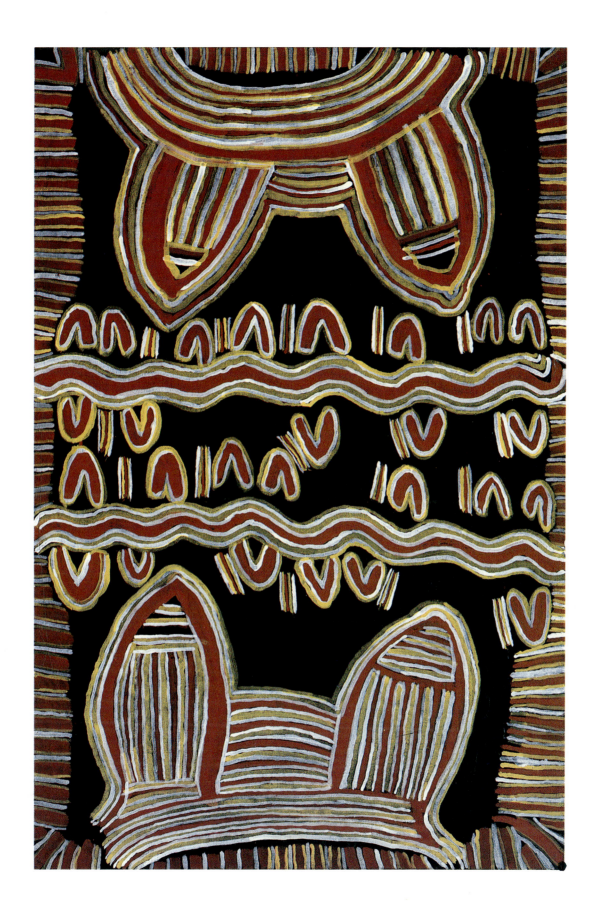

Plate 16
Gloria Petyarre *Awelye* 1989

Plate 17
Gloria Petyarre *Untitled* 1990

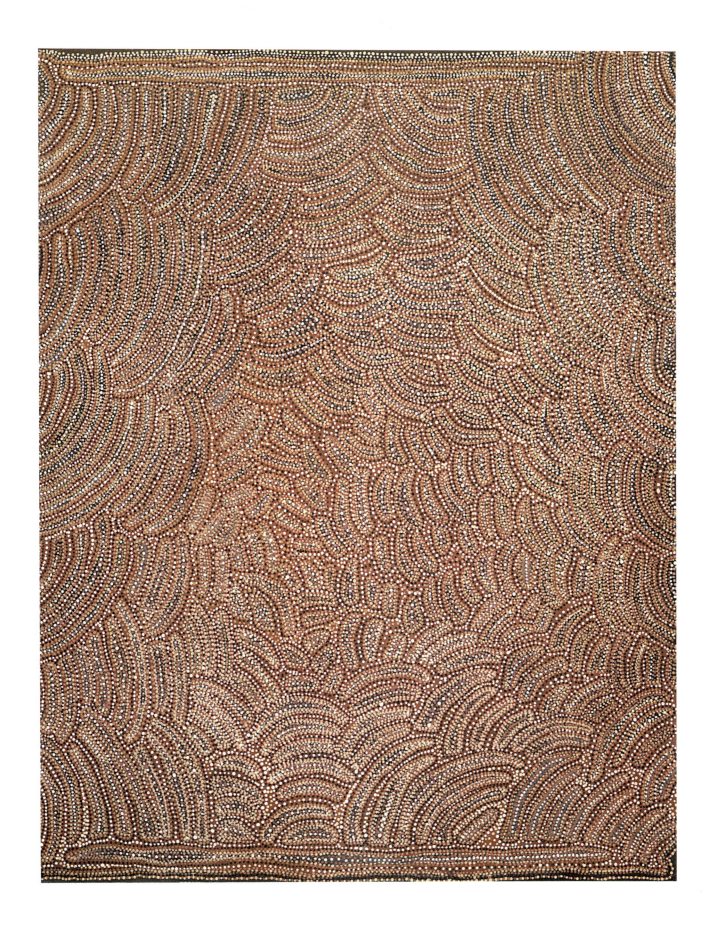

Plate 18
Gloria Petyarre *Sacred Grass* 1990

Plate 19
Kathleen Petyarre *Arnkerrthe Awelye* 1989

Plate 20
Lyndsay Bird Mpetyane *Mulga Apple Dreaming* 1990

Plate 21
Lyndsay Bird Mpetyane *Ceremony* 1989

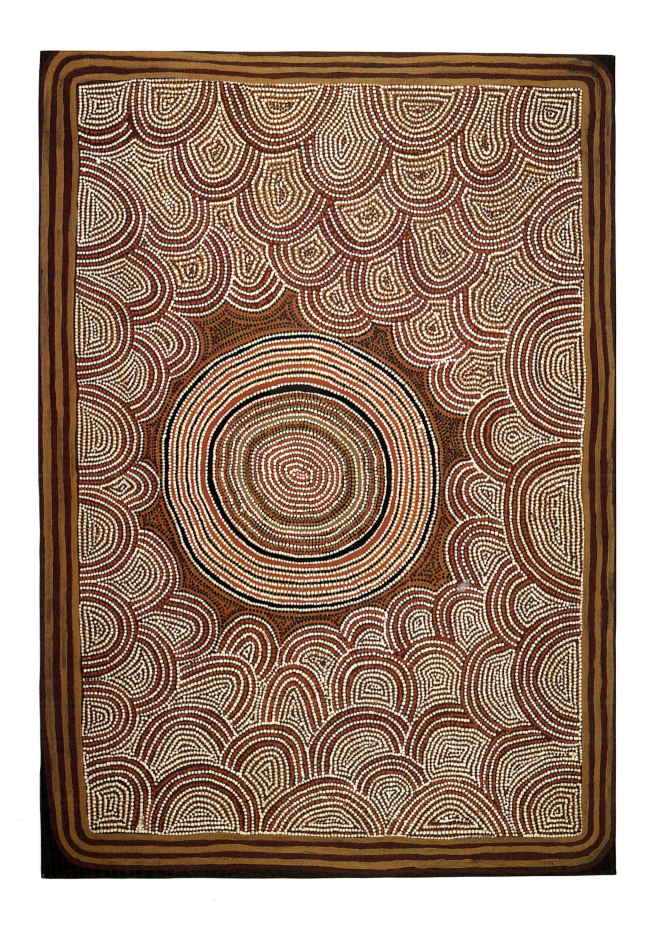

Plate 22
Lyndsay Bird Mpetyane *Wild Bee Dreaming* 1989

Plate 23
Louie Pwerle *Altyerre* 1990

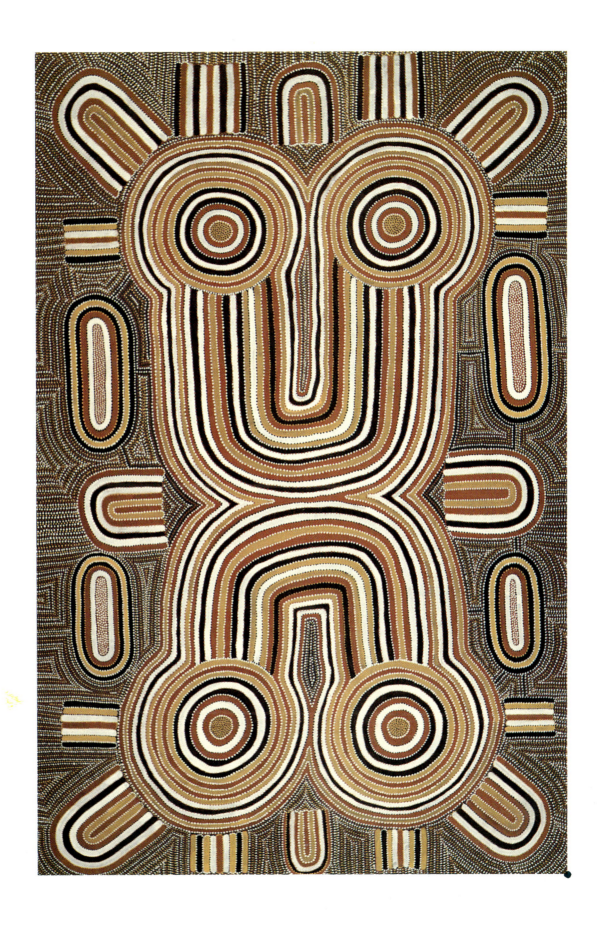

Plate 24
Audrey Kngwarreye *Camp Scene* 1990

Plate 25
Ronnie Price *Untitled* 1990

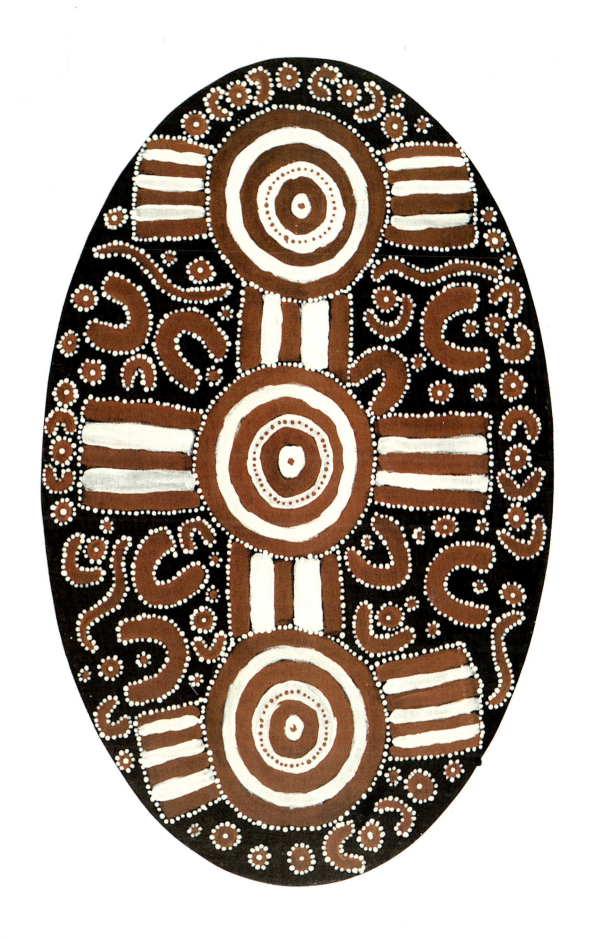

Plate 26
Ada Bird Petyarre *Untitled* 1990

Plate 27
June Bird Petyarre *Untitled* 1990

Plate 28
Ally Kemarre *Bush Flowers* 1989

Plate 29
Tammy Petyarre *Bush Tobacco* 1989

Plate 30
Lena Pwerle *Snake and Honey Ant* 1989

Plate 31
Mavis Holmes Petyarre and May Baily Petyarre *Untitled* 1990

Plate 32
Violet Petyarre *Ngangkare* 1990

Plate 33
Eileen Kngwarreye *Kwertatye* 1990

Plate 34
Lyndsay Bird Mpetyane, Paddy Jungala and Engarlaka *Ilbanda* 1988

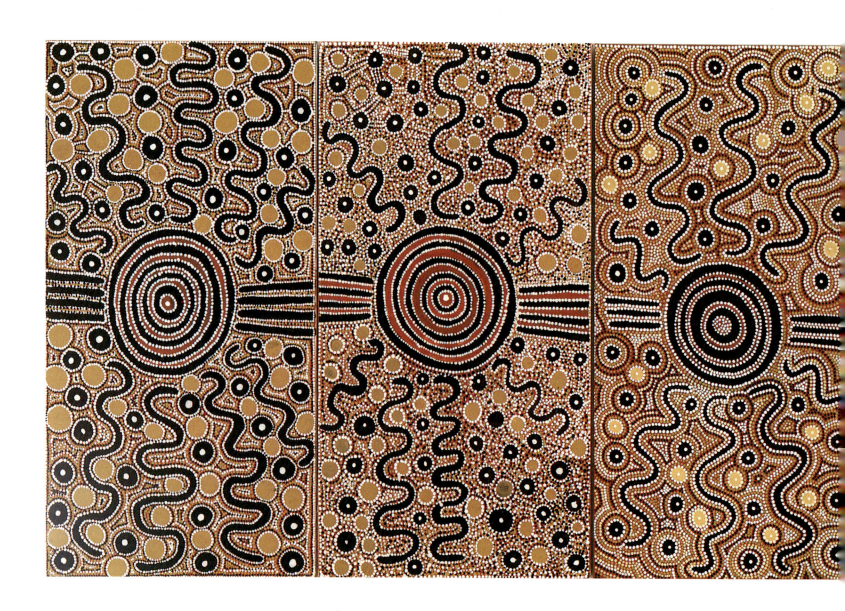

SIX

THE SCULPTURE

The men and women of Utopia have a strong heritage of carving: they have been renowned for their work for a considerable part of this century. They are well represented in museum collections, particularly the South Australian Museum, with artefacts such as boomerangs, shields, spears and coolamons. Their reputation for producing high quality traditional carving is still strong.

Traditional wooden implements are used in daily life. The pieces made for ceremonies, such as shields covered with ochre and black paint, are never placed on the market.

Desert Oak, Kurrajong, Bean and Mulga trees provide the majority of the wood used in sculpting at Utopia. Softwood is much easier to carve, but the hardwood holds finer shapes and detail. In collections of traditional shields from Central Australia, the shields from Utopia are made from softwood because it is lighter. They feature broad, regular, fluted grooves running lengthwise down the face. Shields from further west are traditionally made from hardwood and are covered with much finer detail.

Queenie Kemarre sculpting softwood

Billy Petyarre

Up until the late 1980s, the only non-traditional sculptural work appears to have been done by the women: lizards and animals, some with designs burnt on with hot wire, not unlike those produced by the Pitjantjatjara artists. These works were mainly sold to tourist outlets.

The first significant change came in early 1989 when Janice Kngwarreye, from the Ngkwarlerlaneme community of Utopia, carved a kangaroo and a small male figure (see Plate 45), about 30 centimetres tall. These two pieces were unlike anything that had been carved before — solid, quirky, individual and full of animation. She presented these figures out of the blue: there had been no indication of a change in her approach to carving.

When Rodney Gooch and Christopher Hodges saw these works, they were amazed at how exciting they were. Their highly positive response spawned great activity at Ngkwarlerlaneme. In a very short time a sizeable body of work was produced. One of the recurring sculptural figures has been the *kwertatye*, the ritual law enforcer or, in other guises, the spirit 'bogey' figure. One of the most prolific sculptors of the group, Queenie Kemarre, described one of her *kwertatye* figures, which is now in the Australian National Gallery, to Hodges as:

> … *this is the women who comes out from the site when the girls collect potatoes too close to the sacred site, where they are not supposed to collect. That spirit woman is depicted in a ceremonial situation as a dancer dressed in … makeup*[36].

Some of the other figures from this first period have been described as being of young men, possibly youths painted up before becoming men.

Sculptures of dogs soon followed: squat, solid 'devil devil' dogs and much more lithe camp dogs. The dogs were invariably caught in mid-action, with only three feet on the ground, poised, ready to move. One of the earliest works by senior sculptor Billy Petyarre was a pole with two snakes climbing up it. The subject matter continued to expand.

Rodney Gooch and his staff responded to the upsurge in interest by providing axes, chisels, wood-carving tools, rasps and sandpaper. As noted earlier, acrylic paint was introduced to the Utopia community at large with the canvases for 'A Summer Project', but the sculptors also put it to other uses, adorning every carving they subsequently produced. In an unexpected twist, they began using their sculptures as canvases, onto which beautiful paintings were applied. They mainly used shields which provided an even, if curved, surface.

Up until 1989, the artists were still using traditional earth and ochre colours. On a trip to Alice Springs some of the artists went to the local K-Mart supermarket to buy groceries and noticed some bright acrylic colours for sale. The sculptures that they then produced were covered with bold pinks, reds, greens and blues (see Plate 36).

Non-traditional sculpting spread from Ngkwarlerlaneme when part of the community decided to move closer to Ngkawenyerre, a nearby important site. Sculpting has also spread to Antarrengenye, where Casey Kemarre and Helmut Daly have been carving heads, eagles and lithe, greyhound-like dogs, similar to the camp dogs that live at that outstation.

There is great pride and joy amongst the sculptors, as evidenced by an occasion when Rodney Gooch visited Ngkwarlerlaneme, prior to the establishment of Ngkawenyerre. All the artists were in a very serious mood. Gooch wondered whether there was some dispute or other reason for the people to be acting in such a dour manner. They guided him over to the artists' shed and flung open the door. There lined up in front of him in rows were masses of sculptures, all staring back at him. Everyone burst into laughter. The artists had been so productive, and so pleased with the results, that they had staged a special presentation for him.

THE PLATES

Queenie Kemarre's two figures (Plate 35) are remarkably sensitive works, with an ochre-like application of what is, in fact, acrylic paint.

Billy Petyarre is a senior man at the new camp at Ngkwenyerre. His *Kwertatye Man* (Plate 36) is remarkable for the roundness of the whole form, the lower torso and legs in particular. The upper body of this law enforcer is crossed diagonally with markings that are reminiscent of bandito gunbelts.

Katie Kemarre's *Seated Figure* (Plate 37) has a wide-eyed expression and a boldness in the application of paint. An early piece from 1989, this was the first time that a figure in a position other than standing had been produced by the Utopia sculptors. The way the legs have been formed to deal with the seated position is both quirky and ingenious.

Louie Pwerle's *Kangaroo* (Plate 38) is carved from a single piece of wood from the fork of a tree, enabling the tail to be a continuing part of the sculpture. This technique comes from boomerang making. Pwerle has shown great sensitivity to the form of the animal, whilst the paint allows the form to dominate.

Figure in Shorts and T-shirt (Plate 39) shows Pwerle having fun. This big, blocky human shape has been carved out of very hard mulga wood, and was created at the time of the move to Ngkawenyerre. A number of the sculptors, who made the move at the same time, produced works that had a sense of fun at their core. This perhaps reflected the optimism involved in the establishment of the new camp.

Lucky Kngwarreye's *Possum* (Plate 40) has a simple, elegant form. The colour of the wood is still visible through the painted surface. A spare use of dots allows the purity of the shape to dominate.

A *Devil Devil Dog* (Plate 41) accompanies a *kwertatye* on his or her duties. This sculpture by Billy Petyarre features a bold dotting technique. The dog has its right foot off the ground, in an alert posture waiting and watching. By comparison, Ruby Kngwarreye's *Camp Dog* (Plate 42) has short stumpy legs and a big stumpy tail, which perhaps shows the current preference for this type of bull terrier/pig dog cross amongst her community. The dog is depicted as licking its lips — a good example of the wry humour many of the artists possess.

The figure by Wally Pwerle (Plate 43) was produced with the assistance of his wife Janice Kngwarreye. Working together, they have produced an outstanding body of work that shows their continuing interest in facial expression. Their forms are usually very simple and ordered, with correspondingly structured paintwork which results in remarkably elegant pieces.

Janice Kngwarreye's *Echidna* (Plate 44) was made at the same time as another echidna form; this subject matter has not been repeated by the artist. The body is softwood with holes burnt for the sharpened hardwood sticks that form the spikes. The second sculpture by Kngwarreye (Plate 45) is one of the two pieces that began the non-traditional sculpture movement at Utopia. It is a proud work, produced by a talented sculptor who is skilled in carving techniques — a remarkable first piece.

Queenie Kemarre's *Figure* (Plate 46) is a prime example of her quirky approach to the human form, the body is well-shaped but coloured pale pink, wearing a simple hairstring belt and an enigmatic expression.

Plate 35
Queenie Kemarre *Figures* 1989–90

Plate 36
Billy Petyarre *Kwertatye* 1988

Plate 37
Katie Kemarre *Seated Figure* 1989

Plate 38
Louie Pwerle *Kangaroo* 1989

Plate 39
Louie Pwerle *Figure in Shorts and T-shirt* 1990

Plate 40
Lucky Kngwarreye *Possum* 1989

Plate 41
Billy Petyarre *Devil Devil Dog* 1990

Plate 42
Ruby Kngwarreye *Camp Dog* 1990

Plate 43
Wally Pwerle *Figure* 1990

Plate 44
Janice Kngwarreye *Echidna* 1989

Plate 45
Janice Kngwarreye *Untitled* 1989

Plate 46
Queenie Kemarre *Figure* 1989

Works on Paper

At Utopia, working with fragile material, such as paper, is fraught with difficulties. It is almost impossible to keep paper unmarked and undamaged while the artists are painting. Even in the storage buildings at each camp, paper is susceptible: the culprits are dust and dirt, and they come in an unending supply in the centre of Australia.

Each community outstation is in a cleared area, with buildings congregated around a bore. The bore is the sole source of water. The rivers are dry most of the time since there is very little rainfall. Water is never wasted on growing lawns or ornamental gardens. Therefore, as is the case with most properties owned by whites in the region, the red earth stops at the doorstep, but invariably the dirt does not.

Most outstation buildings on Utopia consist of a verandah which is wide and earthen-floored, sometimes concrete. These verandahs have windbreak sheeting up to about hip-height, with the area above open, but covered by a roof. Inside the buildings proper, there is generally one large room with a smaller room adjacent. The floor here is concrete.

Painting is done outdoors. Only on rare occasions is work done indoors on concrete floors. There are no studios, no stools and no easels. Work is laid flat, on stretchers propped on tins or bed bases, or directly on the ground.

Unlike most of their white counterparts, Aboriginal artists work in a communal environment with frequent interruptions. Songs are sung about the painting in progress. Children are always close by, the older ones watching, listening and learning.

Yet, even given these logistical problems, the Utopia artists, by exercising great care, have been able to work successfully with paper.

Watercolours

Following the success of 'A Summer Project', the next undertaking by the CAAMA Shop and the Utopia artists was a watercolour survey in early 1989.

The Alice Springs region has had a watercolour tradition since the days of Namatjira, but the artists at Utopia had not the same opportunity to work in the medium until the survey. Based on the same premises as 'A Summer Project', watercolour techniques were workshopped and those artists who wanted to participate were supplied with illustration boards, paints and brushes. The survey introduced the artists to yet another medium and gave them the opportunity to explore the techniques available. The survey also served as a trial to see if the illustration boards would survive transport to and from Utopia and the day-to-day rigours of life in the communities.

The result was a remarkable cross-section of the different styles that were developing at Utopia: some artists used the watercolour technique of the Namatjira school; others used the watercolour as a thick paint, not unlike a gouache or matt acrylic. The Robert Holmes à Court Collection acquired the entire survey.

THE PLATES

Joy Petyarre's *Landscape* (Plate 47) is derivative of the Namatjira school, but she has chosen an atypical wet period as the subject. Handling a very new medium, she has very successfully conveyed the brooding, overcast conditions of the time. The abstract of Gladdy Kemarre (Plate 48) is a good example of watercolour being used almost as a gouache in its opaque form. The completely abstracted image relates to paintings done later by Emily Kame Kngwarreye and others, where European eyes see only abstract form.

Myrtle Petyarre with Helen Eager who originated 'The Utopia Suite' and workshopped the wood block techniques with the artists. Note the wood blocks leaning against the bough shelter

Annie Kemarre's work (Plate 49) is strongly influenced by her batik. Bush foods are clearly illustrated amongst the foliage. Again the watercolour has been applied in dense globules. The survey clearly showed an inventiveness with a new medium.

THE UTOPIA SUITE

Christopher Hodges and Helen Eager have played an integral role in introducing new media and materials to the artists.

In February 1990, Hodges and Eager discussed the possibility of a wood block printing survey. The idea had many attractions. The artists were very familiar with carving, and although the final image was on paper, the artists only had to handle durable pieces of wood. Wood block printing is very direct: it captures faithfully each mark made by the artist.

Workshops were held at Utopia during April 1990, during which Hodges and Eager explained the techniques and distributed carving implements and wood blocks to those who wanted to participate. The wood blocks were of a uniform 45 x 30 centimetre size.

The carvings were completed over the next six weeks. In all, 72 woodcut images were returned. It was immediately apparent that the workshops had been successful. The blocks were covered with a wide diversity of marks, from the tiniest scratches to quite deeply gouged areas. The artists had taken images they had used before and translated them to the new medium with outstanding results. Throughout the whole body of work, there are camp scenes and neo-Western landscapes, figurative depictions of lizards, snakes, men with guns, women's and men's ceremonies, and other stylised iconic forms.

'The Utopia Suite' is the largest print survey of an Aboriginal community yet undertaken, and is believed to be the largest group publication of its type produced in Australia.

THE PLATES

Four plates are shown here. The first, by Queenie Kemarre (Plate 50), depicts rocks, people, trees, huts and plants with a delicate patina of grass in the background. Superimposed over these are two sets of women's body paint designs for ceremony. These two images dominate the structure. The second, by Paddy Ngale (Plate 51) is a strong literal image of a group of kangaroos. Within that group there are male kangaroos and females with joeys in their pouches, in amongst dotting and a landscape of little bush flowers. The work by June Bird Petyarre (Plate 52) is of the mountain devil lizard story and pushes the abstract edge of the wood block prints. She has treated the block as an abstract image, with in-fill designs using the tracks of the lizard. Kathleen Petyarre's very naive depiction of a woman (Plate 53) is undoubtedly the most individual and outstanding figurative image of 'The Utopia Suite'. This is a bold and confident work, with a remarkably strong image. The work also succeeds because of the shock of the new.

The blocks for 'The Utopia Suite' are now held by the Australian National Gallery.

SILKSCREENS

The silkscreen project has been evolving since its inception in late 1989 and early 1990. The inherent difficulties of working with paper in a desert environment are never more to the fore than with silkscreen printing: surfaces must be clean. With the help of Eager and Hodges, the artists have learnt to make a master image for the silkscreen. Once completed, the image is then transferred photographically, maintaining the artist's hand in the final work.

Leo Christie of the Cancer Council of New South Wales published a print portfolio in 1988 to raise funds, featuring mainly male, non-Aboriginal artists. The Council then decided to publish a portfolio of women artists in 1990 and thought it would be remiss to not include at least one Aboriginal artist. Christie invited Banduk Marika from Yirrkala in north-east Arnhem Land, and Ada Bird Petyarre from Utopia, to participate.

THE PLATES

The Cancer Council felt Ada Bird Petyarre's *Mountain Devil Lizard* print (Plate 54) was so successful that they commissioned her to do yet another print on the same subject, as an individual print outside the boxed set.

Following the Cancer Council's commission, Gloria Petyarre made a print, *Awelye* (Plate 55), which is featured in the 1991 Australian National Gallery's international calendar. Hodges discussed the silkscreen process with Petyarre at length. She used only three colours in dense fashion and achieved great design simplicity. The red ochre linear pattern depicts the body paint designs for the breasts and the shoulders, and the 'U' shapes are the same women at ceremony. The white dots outlining the red design highlight the structure against the black ground.

Angelina Pwerle's print (Plate 56) is one of a pair, both featuring an old-time ancestor figure. The works have quirky composition, the figures being placed close to the top edge of the paper, making these strange armless figures even more curious.

Plate 47
Joy Petyarre *Landscape* 1989

Plate 48
Gladdy Kemarre *Untitled* 1989

Plate 49
Annie Kemarre *Untitled* 1989

Plate 50
Queenie Kemarre *Untitled* 1990

Plate 51
Paddy Ngale *Untitled* 1990

Plate 52
June Bird Petyarre *Untitled* 1990

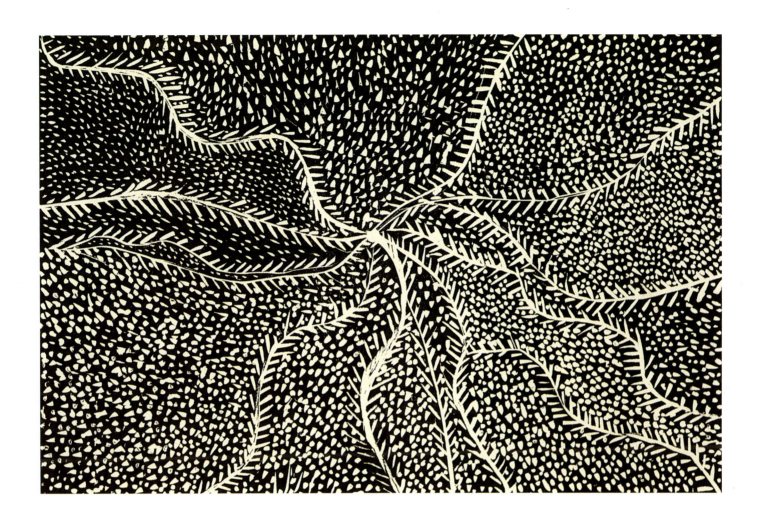

Plate 53
Kathleen Petyarre *Untitled* 1990

Plate 54
Ada Bird Petyarre *Mountain Devil Lizard* 1990

Plate 55
Gloria Petyarre *Awelye* 1990

Plate 56
Angelina Pwerle *Old Time Ancestor* 1990

SPARE-PART ART

The visits to Utopia by Rodney Gooch and Rossi Cole from the CAAMA Shop in Alice Springs take a number of days. The round trip from the southern boundary of Utopia to Alice Springs is nearly 550 kilometres. Once on Utopia there are still considerable distances to be covered, as the outstations are sparsely spread over the 1,800 square kilometres that make up the Utopia Aboriginal Land. Some of the more remote camps are beyond the boundaries, excisions from adjoining properties.

Leaving the relative ease of the tar-sealed Stuart Highway, the so-called Sandover Highway is unsealed: an ochre scar that dissects the landscape from horizon to horizon. The lesser roads and tracks that branch off the Sandover abound with hidden rocks and holes that have the potential to ruin car suspensions, and hardwood stumps and spikes that can quickly flatten a tyre. On just one trip in October 1990, four tyres were shredded. This country is hard on cars.

Canvases, brushes, wood carving tools and other materials from Alice Springs are distributed. The truck is loaded up with new works. There is much delight and excitement as artists show completed canvases, batiks, sculptures and drawings. The journey back to the CAAMA Shop in Alice Springs is inevitably a happy one.

This return trip is normally made at night, and has led to many an animated conversation. Outside is pitch black, save for the headlight beams. Both Gooch and Hodges agree that most of their wild and weird projects have been born from an idea thrashed out during the three to four hour journey.

It was on one of these trips that the BMW art car painted by Michael Tjakamarra Nelson was discussed. Hodges related the background to the commissioning of the BMW art car. There had been considerably conjecture as to which Australian artist should be given the commission. When Michael Nelson's name was mooted as a possibility, he was first asked to paint a car door, in order to see whether his style was suitable. In the end Michael Nelson and a white Australian artist and designer, Ken Done, were both commissioned.

The discussion turned to the many car wrecks that litter the remote roads of the region: where cars have died and been simply abandoned because it is uneconomic to tow them hundreds of kilometres out of the bush. Rather than paint whole cars, the idea was formed to paint just certain parts.

Some time later, staff of CAAMA Shop went back into the bush and unbolted the doors off wrecks, brought them back to Alice Springs, cleaned them up and painted them with rust primer. The doors were taken out to the Antarrengenye outstation, which has developed a tradition of painting neo-Western landscapes of the sites in the region.

Mavis Holmes Petyarre (Plate 57) took to painting one of the car doors with enthusiasm. The body of the door featured a landscape in flattened perspective with a waterhole. But what was surprising was the window, which featured a white man, with red hair and a red beard. There was some apprehension about showing the finished work, but Gooch was very impressed. Anthony Waldegrave Knight, the Melbourne representative of CAAMA, showed the work to William Mora of William Mora Gallery in Melbourne. He was also suitably excited. After discussions with Mora, CAAMA Shop organised the Antarrengenye artists to produce a group show, sufficient for a comprehensive exhibition at the Mora Gallery.

Doors, bonnets and boots from Holdens and Fords were transformed into landscapes that were adapted to the shapes to the car parts. The show 'Art, Cars and the Landscape' attracted national media attention. The Mavis Holmes Petyarre work was acquired by the Australian National Gallery, with the rest of the show acquired by other public institutions and major private collectors.

Whilst such a show can be considered a 'one-off', the spin-offs have been surprisingly important. The Attarrengenye artists have developed confidence from the strong response to the show. They have continued to explore the neo-Western landscapes, that first appeared on their batik work, with outstanding results.

In an interesting follow-on to the 'Art, Cars and the Landscape' exhibition, artists have begun working with hub caps. Ada Bird Petyarre (Plate 58) has painted a hub cap that makes the most of the traditional roundel shapes. The lion shape of the dotted centrepiece, however, gives away the origins of the medium.

Plate 57
Mavis Holmes Petyarre *Untitled* 1990

Plate 58
Ada Bird Petyarre *Hub Cap* 1991

The Aniltji schoolhouse at Boundary
Bore was decorated by the men and
women of the community. The school
sign was painted on a car bonnet

ENDNOTES

1. Interview with Wally Caruana, Curator of Aboriginal Art, Australian National Gallery, November 14, 1990.

2. Australian Bureau of Statistics, 'Census 86 — Australia's Aboriginal and Torres Straits Islander People', Australian Bureau of Statistics, Cat. No. 2503.3, Canberra, 1991, p. 1.

3. *Ibid.* The report quotes the estimate from Butlin, N., *Our Original Aggression: Aboriginal Populations of Southeastern Australia 1788–1850*, George Allen and Unwin, Sydney, 1983.

4. Robert Hughes' article, 'Evoking the Spirit Ancestors', *Time*, October 31, 1988, pp. 79–80.

5. Nadine Amadio *et al.*, *Albert Namatjira: The Life and Work of an Australian Painter*, Macmillan, Melbourne, 1986, p. 2.

6. Wally Caruana interview.

7. This information comes from the map 'Current Distribution of Central Australian Languages', prepared by John Hobson for the Institute of Aboriginal Development Language Centre, Alice Springs and drafted by Julie Carter, 1985 (revised in October, 1988). The producers caution that the map is based on incomplete information. Whilst this information refers to the spread of a particular language group, this does not indicate that a speaker of that language will be found living in full coverage area at any given time.

8. Kathleen Petyarre in Anne Marie Brody's book *Utopia: A Picture Story*, Heytesbury Holdings, Perth, 1990, p. 11.

9. There has been enormous difficulty in expressing the relationship between Aborigines and their land. Mr Justice Woodward, Chairman of the Aboriginal Land Rights Commission (as quoted by Kenneth Maddock in Peterson N. & Langton M. (eds.), *Aborigines, Land and Land Rights*, Australian Institute of Aboriginal Studies, Canberra, 1983, p. 215 says: 'The problem of understanding is made worse by … the difficulty of expressing many Aboriginal ideas and arrangements in English terms … Further, some Aboriginal concepts related to land-owning have no parallel in European law.' (ALRC 1973: 11–12; 1974: 135–136).

10. This is only a very cursory explanation of the Dreaming. It is a term that cannot be easily explained. Every book on the subject seems to proffer another variant. The endless dilemma of the relationship between Aboriginal and white Australian, seems to hinge on the desire of white people to simplify their understanding of the complexity of Aboriginal society and culture.

11. *Kaititja* was the spelling current at the time of the land claim hearing, but is now spelt *Kaytetye.*

12. Meredith Rowell in Peterson N. and Langton M. (eds.), *Aborigines, Land and Land Rights*, Australian Institute of Aboriginal Studies, Canberra, 1983, p. 259.

13. Toohey J., 'Report to the Minister for Aboriginal Affairs of the Land Claim by the Anmatjirra and Alyawarra to the Utopia Pastoral Lease', Canberra, 1980.

14. Interview with Julia Murray, February 18, 1991.

15. Interview with Rodney Gooch, October 25, 1990.

16. Galarrwuy Yanupingu in Caruana, Wally (ed.), *Windows on the Dreaming: Aboriginal Paintings in the Australian National Gallery*, Australian National Gallery and Ellsyd Press, Canberra, 1989, pp. 13–14.

17. Kathleen Petyarre quoted in Brody A.M., *Utopia: A Picture Story*, Heytesbury Holdings, Perth, 1980, p. 12.

18. The information here is based on two interviews conducted by the author: Julia Murray on February 18, 1991 and Jenny Green on March 12, 1991.

19. Julia Murray interview.

20. *Ibid.*

21. *Ibid.*

22. Rodney Gooch in Brody, A.M., *Utopia: A Picture Story*, Heytesbury Holdings, Perth, 1990, p. 7.

23. Rodney Gooch interview, October 25, 1990.

24. Interview with Christopher Hodges, December 7, 1990.

25. Interview with Anne Marie Brody, November 29, 1990.

26. Interview with Christopher Hodges.

27. See p.25

28. Julia Murray interview.

29. Anne Maria Brody interview.

30. Brody A.M., *Utopia: A Picture Story*, Heytesbury Holdings, Perth, 1990, p. 19.

31. See Chapter 3, 'The Art Tradition', in this book

32. Christopher Hodges interview

33. See 'List of Exhibitions', for details.

34. Courtesy of CAAMA Shop.

35. Christopher Heathcote argues a similar case in 'Spirit in Land', *Art Monthly Australia*, March 1991, No. 38, Canberra, pp. 13–14.

36. Interview with Christopher Hodges, December 7, 1990.

LIST OF PLATES

1. Gloria Petyarre, *Awelye*, 1989, batik on silk, 100 x 100 cm. irreg. Private collection

2. Emily Kame Kngwarreye, *Untitled*, 1988, batik on silk, 180 x 90 cm. irreg. Private collection

3. Rosemary Petyarre, *Untitled*, 1990, batik on silk, 180 x 100 cm. irreg. Collection: Barbara Eager

4. Lena Pwerle, *Untitled*, 1990, batik on silk, 180 x 100 cm. irreg. Courtesy: Utopia Art Sydney

5. Ruby Kngwarreye, *Untitled*, 1988, batik on silk, 100 x 100 cm. irreg. Private collection

6. Mavis Holmes Petyarre, *Untitled*, 1989, batik on silk, 118 x 122 cm. Private collection

7. Edie Kemarre, *Untitled*, 1988, batik on silk, 100 x 100 cm. irreg. Private collection

8. Mavis Petyarre, *Flock Pigeon Dreaming* from 'Utopia: A Picture Story', 1989, batik on silk, 250 x 120 cm. irreg. Collection: The Robert Holmes à Court Collection

9. Lyndsay Bird Mpetyane, *Men's Ceremony*, 1988, batik on silk, 180 x 90 cm. irreg. Private collection

10. Julie Purvis Mpetyane, *Bush Potato Dreaming* from 'Utopia: A Picture Story', 1989, batik on silk, 250 x 120 cm. irreg. Collection: The Robert Holmes à Court Collection

11. Emily Kame Kngwarreye, *Emu Woman*, 1988–1989, 'Utopia Women's Paintings: The First Works on Canvas, A Summer Project 1988–89', synthetic polymer on linen, 92 x 61 cm. Collection: The Robert Holmes à Court Collection

12. Emily Kame Kngwarreye, *Untitled*, 1990, synthetic polymer on linen, 97 x 116 cm. irreg. Private collection

13. Emily Kame Kngwarreye, *Intekwe (Pareke)*, 1990, synthetic polymer on linen, 130 x 231 cm. Collection: Allen Allen & Hemsley

14. Ada Bird Petyarre, *Bush Yam Awelye*, 1990, synthetic polymer on linen, 135 x 135 cm. Courtesy of Utopia Art Sydney

15. Ada Bird Petyarre, *Ntange Awelye*, 1988–89, 'Utopia Women's Paintings: The First Works on Canvas, A Summer Project 1988–89', synthetic polymer on linen, 92 x 61 cm. Collection: The Robert Holmes à Court Collection

16. Gloria Petyarre, *Awelye*, 1989, synthetic polymer on linen, 150 x 120 cm. Private collection

17. Gloria Petyarre, *Untitled*, 1990, synthetic polymer on linen, 150 x 120 cm. Private collection

18. Gloria Petyarre, *Sacred Grass*, 1990, synthetic polymer on linen, 100 x 100 cm. Courtesy: Utopia Art Sydney

19. Kathleen Petyarre, *Arnkerrthe Awelye*, 1989, synthetic polymer on linen, 135 x 135 cm. Private collection

20. Lyndsay Bird Mpetyane, *Mulga Apple Dreaming*, 1990, synthetic polymer on linen, four panels: each 22 x 100 cm. Collection: Australian National Gallery, Canberra

21. Lyndsay Bird Mpetyane, *Ceremony*, 1989, synthetic polymer on linen, 119 x 166 cm. Courtesy: Utopia Art Sydney

22. Lyndsay Bird Mpetyane, *Wild Bee Dreaming*, 1989, synthetic polymer on linen, 135 x 135 cm. Private collection

23. Louie Pwerle, *Altyerre*, 1990, synthetic polymer on linen, 180 x 120 cm. Courtesy: Utopia Art Sydney

24. Audrey Kngwarreye, *Camp Scene*, 1990, synthetic polymer on linen, 100 x 100 cm. Private collection

25. Ronnie Price, *Untitled*, 1990, from the Body Paint Design Collection, synthetic polymer on linen, oval: 54 x 85 cm. Courtesy: CAAMA Shop, Alice Springs

26. Ada Bird Petyarre, *Untitled*, 1990, from the Body Paint Design Collection, synthetic polymer on linen, oval: 54 x 85 cm. Courtesy: CAAMA Shop, Alice Springs

27. June Bird Petyarre, *Untitled*, 1990, from the Body Paint Design Collection, synthetic polymer on linen, oval: 54 x 85 cm. Courtesy: CAAMA Shop, Alice Springs

28. Ally Kemarre, *Bush Flowers*, 1989, synthetic polymer on linen, 90 x 60 cm. Private collection

29. Tammy Petyarre, *Bush Tobacco*, 1989 synthetic polymer on linen, 90 x 60 cm. Private collection

30. Lena Pwerle, *Snake and Honey Ant*, 1989, synthetic polymer on linen, 60 x 120 cm. Collection: Rhondda Findleton

31. Mavis Holmes Petyarre and May Baily Petyarre, *Untitled*, 1990, synthetic polymer on linen, 4 panels, each 120 x 60 cm. Collection: Beverley and Anthony Waldegrave Knight

32. Violet Petyarre, *Ngangkare*, 1990, from the Body Paint Design Series, synthetic polymer on board, 45 x 30 cm. Private collection

33. Eileen Kngwarreye, *Kwertatye*, 1990, from the Body Paint Design Series, synthetic polymer on board, 45 x 30 cm. Private collection

34. Lyndsay Bird Mpetyane, Paddy Jungala and Engarlaka, *Ilbanda*, 1988, synthetic polymer on linen, six panels, each 140 x 73 cm. Collection: Austral Gallery, St Louis, USA

35. Queenie Kemarre, *Figures*, 1989/90, synthetic polymer on bean wood, h. 49 cm, h. 45 cm. Private collection

36. Billy Petyarre, *Kwertatye*, 1988, synthetic polymer on bean wood, h. 87 cm. Private collection

37. Katie Kemarre, *Seated Figure*, 1989, synthetic polymer on bean wood, h. 81 cm. Private collection

38. Louie Pwerle, *Kangaroo*, 1989, synthetic polymer on softwood, h. 76 cm. Private collection

39. Louie Pwerle, *Figure in Shorts and T-shirt*, 1990, synthetic polymer on mulga wood, h. 93 cm. Private collection

40. Lucky Kngwarreye, *Possum*, 1989, synthetic polymer on hardwood, l. 69 cm. Private collection

41. Billy Petyarre, *Devil Devil Dog*, 1990, synthetic polymer on softwood, l. 82 cm. Collection: Michael Boulter and Libby Slater

42. Ruby Kngwarreye, *Camp Dog*, 1990, synthetic polymer on softwood, l. 54 cm. Collection: Gregory Dawes

43. Wally Pwerle, *Figure*, 1990, synthetic polymer on hardwood, h. 120 cm. Collection: The Robert Holmes à Court Collection

44. Janice Kngwarreye, *Echidna*, 1989, synthetic polymer on wood. Collection: James and Lynda Eager

45. Janice Kngwarreye, *Untitled*, 1989, synthetic polymer on bean wood, h. 40 cm. Private collection

46. Queenie Kemarre, *Figure*, 1989, synthetic polymer on hardwood, h. 76 cm. Courtesy: Utopia Art Sydney

47. Joy Petyarre, *Landscape*, 1989, watercolour on illustration board, 25.3 x 38 cm. Collection: The Robert Holmes à Court Collection

48. Gladdy Kemarre, *Untitled*, 1989, watercolour on illustration board, 25.3 x 38.1 cm. Collection: The Robert Holmes à Court Collection

49. Annie Kemarre, *Untitled*, 1989, watercolour on illustration board, 25.4 x 38.2 cm. Collection: The Robert Holmes à Court Collection

50. Queenie Kemarre, *Untitled*, 1990, from the Utopia Suite, woodcut on paper, 45 x 30 cm. Courtesy: Utopia Art Sydney

51. Paddy Ngale, *Untitled*, 1990, from the Utopia Suite, woodcut on paper, 45 x 30 cm. Courtesy: Utopia Art Sydney

52. June Bird Petyarre, *Untitled*, 1990, from the Utopia Suite, woodcut on paper, 45 x 30 cm. Courtesy: Utopia Art Sydney

53. Kathleen Petyarre, *Untitled*, 1990, from the Utopia Suite, woodcut on paper, 45 x 30 cm. Courtesy: Utopia Art Sydney

54. Ada Bird Petyarre, *Mountain Devil Lizard*, 1990, silkscreen on paper, 76 x 56 cm. From the Cancer Council of New South Wales, The 1990 Collection: *A Portfolio of Australian Women Artists*

55. Gloria Petyarre, *Awelye*, 1990, silkscreen on paper, 76 x 56 cm. Published by Utopia Art Sydney

56. Angelina Pwerle, *Old Time Ancestor*, 1990, silkscreen on paper, 76 x 56 cm. Published by Utopia Art Sydney

57. Mavis Holmes Petyarre, *Untitled*, 1990, synthetic polymer on car door, 99 x 105 cm irreg. Collection: Australian National Gallery, Canberra

58. Ada Bird Petyarre, *Hub Cap*, 1991, synthetic polymer on hub cap, 27 cm. dia. Courtesy: Utopia Art Sydney

EXHIBITIONS

1991   'Utopia Batik', Utopia Art Sydney, Sydney
        'Long Hot Summer', Utopia Art Sydney, Sydney
        'A Picture Story', Meat Market Gallery, Melbourne
        'Camp Scenes', The Gallery at the Prince and Frog, Melbourne

1990   'A Picture Story' Tandanya Centre, Adelaide; The Royal Hibernian Academy, Dublin
        'Utopia Men and Dogs', Austral Gallery, St Louis, USA
        'CAAMA/Utopia Artists-in-Residence Project: Louie Pwerle and Emily Kame Kngwarreye',
            Perth Institute of Contemporary Art, Perth
        'Art from Utopia', Orange Regional Gallery, Orange, NSW
        'The Figure', Utopia Art Sydney, Sydney
        'Utopia Artists', Flinders Lane Gallery, Melbourne
        'Art, Cars and the Landscape', William Mora Galleries, Melbourne
        'New Year — New Art', Utopia Art Sydney, Sydney
        'The New Images of Utopia', Gallery Gundulmirri, Warrandyte, Victoria

1989   'Utopia', Utopia Art Sydney, Sydney
        'Utopia Women', Coventry Gallery, Sydney
        'Paintings from Utopia', Austral Gallery, St Louis, USA
        'Twelve Men and an Echidna', Utopia Art Sydney, Sydney
        'Aboriginal Art Now', New England Regional Art Museum, Armidale, NSW
        'Utopia Batik', Araleun Art Centre, Alice Springs
        'Utopia Batik', Darwin Museum and Gallery, Darwin
        'A Summer Project: Utopia Women's Paintings (The First Works on Canvas), S.H. Ervin
            Museum, Sydney; Orange Regional Gallery, Orange, NSW
        'Aboriginal Art from Utopia', Gallery Gabrielle Pizzi, Melbourne

1988   'Time Before Time', Austral Gallery, St Louis, USA
        'Painting and Batik from the Desert', Utopia Art Sydney, Sydney
        'Utopia Batik', Craft Council of Australia Gallery, Canberra

1987   Fremantle Arts Centre, Fremantle
        Darwin Museum Gallery, Darwin
        Yirrkala Community Centre, Yirrkala, NT
        Jogjakarta Fine Art Academy, Jogjakarta
        Sydney Expo, Craft Council of NSW Gallery, Sydney
        Araluen Arts Centre, Alice Springs

1986   Craft Council of Australia Gallery, Canberra
        Bundaberg Art Gallery, Bundaberg, Queensland
        Araluen Arts Centre, Alice Springs

1985   'Black Women in Focus', Adelaide Festival, Adelaide
        Burnie Gallery, Burnie, Tasmania
        Tasmanian Craft Council Gallery, Hobart

1984   Craft Council of Australia Gallery, Canberra
        Queensland University Gallery, Brisbane
        Fireworks Gallery, Adelaide
        Sydney Craft Expo, Sydney
        Darwin Craft Council Gallery, Darwin
        Araluen Arts Centre, Alice Springs

1983   Adelaide Festival Centre, Adelaide
        Alice Springs Craft Council, Alice Springs

1982   Sydney Craft Expo, Sydney
        Brisbane Commonwealth Games Exhibition, Brisbane

1981   'Floating Forests of Silk: Utopia Batik from the Desert', Adelaide Festival Centre, Adelaide

1980   'Artworks', Mona Byrnes Gallery, Gillen, Alice Springs

GROUP EXHIBITIONS

1991   'Aboriginal Art and Spirituality', High Court of Australia, Canberra
        'Contemporary Aboriginal Art', Art Gallery of NSW, Sydney
        'Australian Perspecta 1991', Art Gallery of NSW, Sydney

1990   'Contemporary Aboriginal Art', Carpenter Center, Harvard University, Boston
        'Tangari Lia: My Family', Third Eye Centre, Glasgow
        'A.C.A.F.2 — The Second Australian Contemporary Art Fair', Exhibition Centre,
            Melbourne
        'Gold Coast Festival of Sculpture', Gold Coast City Art Gallery, Surfers Paradise,
            Queensland
        'Ten Women Artists', Macquarie Galleries, Sydney
        'The Last Show', Utopia Art Sydney, Sydney

1989   'A Continuing Tradition', Australian National Gallery, Canberra
        'Mythscapes', National Gallery of Victoria, Melbourne
        'Fashion: A Contemporary Art', Victoria and Albert Museum, London;
            Powerhouse Museum, Sydney
        'Arts of Australia, Indonesia and India', May Weber Museum, Chicago
        'A Myriad of Dreamings', Westpac Gallery, Melbourne
        'Contemporary Aboriginal Art', Bloomfield Galleries, Sydney

1988   'Aboriginal Art Now', New England Regional Art Museum, Armidale, NSW
        'The Inspired Dream', Queensland Art Gallery, Brisbane
        'Contemporary Aboriginal Art', Utopia Art Sydney, Sydney
        'Peintures Aborigines', Arte Productions, Paris

SOLO EXHIBITIONS

1991   Gloria Petyarre, Utopia Art Sydney, Sydney
        Lyndsay Bird Mpetyane, Utopia Art Sydney, Sydney
        Emily Kame Kngwarreye, Utopia Art Sydney, Sydney
        Lily Sandover Kngwarreye, The Gallery at the Price and Frog, Melbourne

1990   Emily Kame Kngwarreye, Utopia Art Sydney, Sydney
        Ada Bird Petyarre, Utopia Art Sydney
        Louie Pwerle, Utopia Art Sydney, Sydney

1989   Lyndsay Bird Mpetyane, Syme-Dodson Gallery in association with Utopia Art Sydney,
            Sydney

BOOKS AND CATALOGUES

Amadio, Nadine & Kimber, Richard *Wildbird Dreaming: Aboriginal Art from the Central Deserts of Australia*, Greenhouse, Melbourne, 1988

Amadio, Nadine *et al. Albert Namatjira: The Life and Work of an Australian Painter*, Macmillan Australia, Melbourne, 1986

Australian Bureau of Statistics *Census 86 – Australia's Aboriginal and Torres Strait Islander People*, Australian Bureau of Statistics Cat. No. 2503. 0, Canberra, 1991

Author Unknown *The CAAMA Group*, CAAMA Group of Companies, Alice Springs, 1989

Baglin, Douglass & Moore, David R. *People of the Dreamtime: The Australian Aborigines*, Walker/Weatherhill, New York, 1970

Bardon, Geoff *Aboriginal Art of the Western Desert*, Rigby, Adelaide, 1979

Batty, Philip & Gooch, Rodney *CAAMA/Utopia Artists-in-Residence Project: Louie Pwerle and Emily Kame Kngwarreye, 1989–1990*, Perth Institute of Contemporary Arts, Perth, 1990

Beier, Ulli (ed.) 'Long Water: Aboriginal Art and Literature — A Special Issue of Aspect', *Aspect 34*, Aboriginal Artists Agency & Aspect, August 1986

Bell, Diane *Daughters of the Dreaming*, McPhee Gribble/George Allen & Unwin, Sydney, 1983

Berndt, R.M. & C.H. *The First Australians*, Ure Smith, Sydney, 1974 (3rd. ed.)

Berndt, R.M. & C.H. with Stanton, John E. *Aboriginal Australian Art: A Visual Perspective*, Methuen Australia, Melbourne, 1982

Boulter, Michael *Ada Bird Petyarre: Painting, Sculpture, Batik, Prints* (exhibition catalogue), Utopia Art Sydney, Sydney, 1990

Boulter, Michael *Emily Kame Kngwarreye* (exhibition catalogue), Utopia Art Sydney, Sydney, 1990

Boulter, Michael & Hodges, Christopher *Australia's First International Art Movement*, Utopia Art Sydney, Sydney, 1990

Brody, Anne Marie *Contemporary Aboriginal Art from The Robert Holmes à Court Collection*, Heytesbury Holdings, Perth, 1990

Brody, Anne Marie *The Face of the Centre: Papunya Tula Paintings 1971–84*, National Gallery of Victoria, 1985

Brody, Anne Marie *Utopia: A Picture Story*, Heytesbury Holdings, Perth, 1990

Brody, Anne Marie *Utopia, A Picture Story: 88 Works on Silk*, Aboriginal Cultural Institute, Adelaide, 1989

Brody, Anne Marie *Utopia Women's Painting: The First Works on Canvas, A Summer Project 1988–1989* (exhibition catalogue), Heytesbury Holdings, Perth, 1989

Caruana, Wally (ed.) *Windows on the Dreaming: Aboriginal Paintings in the Australian National Gallery*, Australian National Gallery/Ellsyd Press, Canberra, 1989

Cooper, Carol *et al. Australian Aborigines* (exhibition catalogue), Australian Gallery Directors Council, Canberra, 1981

Edwards, Robert (ed.) *Aboriginal Art in Australia*, Ure Smith, Sydney, 1978

Edwards, Robert & Guerin, Bruce *Aboriginal Bark Paintings*, Rigby, Adelaide, 1969

Elkin, A.P. *et al. The Australian Aborigines*, The Department of Territories, Canberra, 1967

Godden, Elaine & Malnic, Jutta *Rock Paintings of Aboriginal Australia*, Reed Books, Sydney, 1988

Harney, W.E. & Elkin, A.P. *Songs of the Songmen*, Cheshire, Melbourne, 1949

Hodges, Christopher *Utopia Women* (exhibition catalogue), Coventry Gallery, Sydney, 1989

Isaacs, Jennifer *Australian Aboriginal Paintings*, Weldon Publishing, Sydney, 1989

Isaacs, Jennifer *Australia's Living Heritage: Arts of the Dreaming*, Landsdowne Press, Sydney, 1984

Kean, John (curator) *East to West: Land in Papunya Tula Painting*, The Aboriginal Cultural Institute, Adelaide, 1990

Maughan, Janet & Zimmer, Jenny *Dot & Circle: A Retrospective Survey of the Aboriginal Acrylic Paintings of Central Australia*, Royal Melbourne Institute of Technology, Melbourne, 1986

Peterson, Nicholas & Marcia Langton (eds.) *Aborigines, Land and Land Rights*, Australian Institute of Aboriginal Studies, Canberra, 1983

Pizzi, Gabrielle *Contemporary Paintings from Papunya Tula*, Gallery Gabrielle Pizzi, Melbourne, 1989

Premont, Roslyn & Lennard, Mark *Tjukurrpa: Desert Paintings of Central Australia*, Centre for Aboriginal Artists, Alice Springs, 1988

Ryan, Judith *Mythscapes: Aboriginal Art of the Desert from the National Gallery of Victoria*, Melbourne, 1989

Ryan, Judith *Paint Up Big: Warlpiri Women's Art of Lajamanu*, National Gallery of Victoria, Melbourne, 1990

Sutton, Peter (ed.) *Dreamings: The Art of Aboriginal Australia*, The Asia Society of Galleries, New York in association with George Braziller, New York, 1988

West, Margie K.C. *The Inspired Dream: Life as Art in Aboriginal Australia*, Museums and Art Galleries of the Northern Territory, with the Queensland Art Gallery, Brisbane, 1988

ARTICLES

Batty, Philip 'Money, Corruption and Authenticity: What is Authentic Aboriginal Art?' *Artlink*, Autumn/Winter 1990, Vol. 10, nos. 1–2, pp. 32–33

Boulter, Michael 'Contemporary Aboriginal art prices hold firm', Utopia Art Sydney, July 26, 1990

Boulter, Michael 'Invasion of the Ngkwarlerlaneme People', Utopia Art Sydney, May 26, 1990

Green, Jenny (ed.) 'Utopia: Women Country and Batik', exhibition catalogue, Adelaide Festival Centre Gallery, Adelaide, SA 1981

Green, Jenny 'Country in Mind: Life after Namatjira', *Artlink*, Autumn/Winter 1990, Vol 10. nos 1–2, pp. 12–13

Grzybowicz, Neva 'Kinship and the Dreaming', *Artlink*, Autumn/Winter 1990, Vol. 10, nos. 1–2, p. 29

Hannaford, Kay 'Tandanya: Australia's First Aboriginal Cultural Institute', *Artlink*, Autumn/Winter 1990, Vol. 10, nos. 1–2, pp. 106–107

Heathcote, Christopher 'Spirit in Land', *Art Monthly Australia*, March 1991, No. 38, Canberra, pp. 13–14

Hodges, Christopher 'Utopia: from Song to Batik to Canvas, a Remarkable Journey', *Artlink*, Autumn/Winter 1990, Vol. 10, nos. 1–2, pp. 9–10

Hughes, Robert 'Evoking the Spirit Ancestors', *Time*, October 31, 1988, pp. 79–80

McDonald, John 'Black Funk Warms a Cool Culture', *Sydney Morning Herald*, April 20, 1988, p. 20

Mendelssohn, Joanna 'Paintings from Utopia', *The Bulletin*, May 16, 1989, p. 118

Rae, Michael 'Superstar or Generic?', *Artlink*, Autumn/Winter 1990, Vol. 10, nos. 1–2, pp. 36–37

Stephens, Tony 'Fame Finds Emily at Borehole', *Sydney Morning Herald*, April 23, 1990, p. 2

Taylor, Paul 'Primitive Dreams are Hitting the Big Time', *New York Times*, May 21, 1989, pp. 30, 31, 35

Thompson, Sylvia 'The Dreaming of a Whole Continent', *The Irish Times*, August 22, 1990, pp. 8–9

Watson, Bronwyn 'Women Cast Their Eyes Over Utopia', *Sydney Morning Herald*, April 15, 1989, p. 92

West, Margie 'The Law and Women: New Custodianships and Responsibilities', *Artlink*, Autumn/Winter 1990, Vol. 10, nos. 1–2, p. 26

PHOTOGRAPHIC CREDITS

COLOUR PLATES

All colour plates photographed by Christopher Hodges and Helen Eager except for

Plates 8, 10, 11, 15, 47, 48, 49 courtesy The Robert Holmes à Court Collection;
Plate 6 courtesy Coventry Gallery, Sydney
Plate 13 photographed by Raye Woodbury
Plate 31 photographed by Henry Jolles, courtesy Alcaston House Gallery, Melbourne
Plates 32, 33 courtesy Elaine Kitchener
Plate 37 courtesy Austral Galleries, St Louis, Missouri
Plate 57 photographed by John Brash, courtesy William Mora Galleries

BLACK AND WHITE PHOTOGRAPHS

All black and white photographs by Michael Boulter except for
pp. 17, 18, 31, 34 photographed by John Corker
p. 25 courtesy of Jenny Green
pp. 27 and 35 courtesy of Julia Murray
pp. 59, 64, 114, 141, 168 photographed by Christopher Hodges
Where applicable, copyright remains with photographer.

INDEX